Michigan's
State Forests

❧

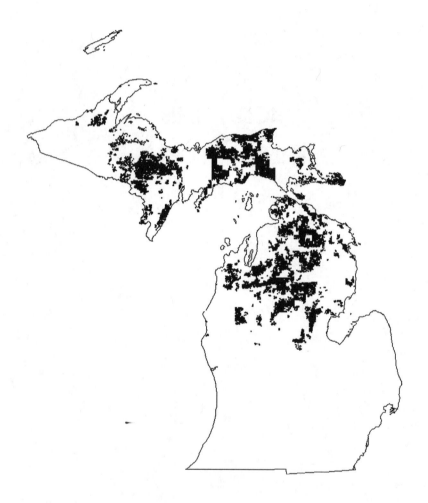

Currently, more than ten percent of Michigan's land area is found within its managed state forest system. The fascinating story of their origin, growth, protection and management is a testimony to the skills, dedication and commitment of the professional foresters who led the effort for over 100 years.

Used courtesy of Larry A. Leefers, Michigan State University Department of Forestry. Source is the Michigan Department of Natural Resources and the Michigan Geographic Data Library, Michigan Department of Information Technology, 2005.

Michigan's State Forests

A CENTURY OF STEWARDSHIP

William B. Botti *and* Michael D. Moore

Michigan State University Press • *East Lansing*

♾ The paper used in this publication meets the minimum requirements of ANSI/NISO
Z39.48-1992 (R 1997) (Permanence of Paper).

 Michigan State University Press
East Lansing, Michigan 48823-5245
www.msupress.msu.edu

Printed and bound in the United States of America.

12 11 10 09 08 07 06   1 2 3 4 5 6 7 8 9 10

LIBRARY OF CONGRESS CATALOGING-IN-PUBLICATION DATA
Botti, William B.
Michigan's state forests : a century of stewardship / William B. Botti and
Michael D. Moore.
p. cm. — (Dave Dempsey environmental series)
Includes bibliographical references and index.
ISBN-13: 978-0-87013-780-8 (pbk. 13dig : alk. paper)
ISBN-10: 0-87013-780-8 (pbk. 10dig : alk. paper)
1. Forests and forestry—Michigan—History. 2. Forest management—Michigan—History. I.
Moore, Michael D. II. Title. III. Series: Dave Dempsey environmental series
SD144.M5B68 2006
333.75'1609774—dc22
2006021696

Book and cover design by Sharp Des!gns, Inc.

All pen and ink drawings are the work of William B. Botti, all rights reserved.
Cover photograph is used courtesy of the Michigan Department of Natural Resources.

The authors may be contacted via e-mail at *bottiw1@juno.com* and *mdmoore817@aol.com*

g green Michigan State University Press is a member of the Green Press Initiative and is
press committed to developing and encouraging ecologically responsible publishing
INITIATIVE
practices. For more information about the Green Press Initiative and the use of recycled paper
in book publishing, please visit *www.greenpressinitiative.org*.

Visit Michigan State University Press on the World Wide Web at *www.msupress.msu.edu*

DEDICATION

THIS BOOK IS DEDICATED TO THE MEN AND WOMEN OF THE MICHIGAN state forest management system. Their devotion, commitment, hard work, and professionalism for more than one hundred years have made Michigan's state forest system a crown jewel in the Great Lakes State. They and they alone are responsible for taking these largely abandoned cutover, exhausted, and burned-over lands and through loving care creating a great economic, ecological, and recreational asset for the people of the state of Michigan. The scientific application of sustainable forestry practices by generations of foresters, technicians, and other professionals has created the wonderful state forest system we have today.

❧

❧

"Advice to persons about to write history—Don't."
LORD ACTON, 1887

❧

"History is not a schoolmistress. . . . She is a prison
matron who punishes for unlearned lessons."

VASILY KLYUTCHEVSKY, RUSSIAN HISTORIAN

❧

"We can chart our future clearly and wisely only when
we know the path which has led to the present."

ADLAI STEVENSON, 1952

❧

"A nation must believe in three things: It must believe in the past.
It must believe in the future. It must, above all, believe in the
capacity of its own people so to learn from the past that they
can gain in judgment for the creation of the future."

FRANKLIN D. ROOSEVELT, 1941

Contents

Acknowledgments

THE AUTHORS ARE FORESTERS WHO LOVE HISTORY, NOT HISTORIANS with an affinity for forestry. The authors consequently are indebted to many individuals—most of them foresters and other natural resources professionals—for their encouragement and sharing of information. We especially thank author and environmental specialist David Dempsey, who not only provided editing of the text but pushed, prodded, and encouraged the authors during the entire journey.

We also thank former colleague Ted Reuschel, who read the text and pointed out many areas for improvement. Longtime executive assistant Wanda Stevens was always available to dig out some obscure information from the files. Former district forester Jack Lockwood contributed material of great interest.

Others who provided assistance include John Gaffney, Peter Grieves, the late Carlton Hollister, Dr. Larry Leefers, William Mahalak, Glenn Schaap, Clayton Schooley, Dr. Jerry Thiede, and Don Zettle.

A heartfelt thanks goes to the late Harold Kollmeyer, a longtime colleague who preserved much of the source material for this effort. Without his commitment to preserving historical material, much of the heritage of the state forests would have been lost forever.

Both authors are indebted to the many secretaries, technicians, biologists and other professional and support personnel that they worked with over the years. Their strong support, dedication and friendship greatly contributed to the joy of working for the Michigan Department of Natural Resources.

Bill Botti offers special thanks to all those who supervised him throughout his thirty-two years' work in the state forest system—Robert A. Borak, the late Paul R. Flink, James L. Halbach, Ernest C. Hall, the late Arne A. Metsa, Theodore M. Reuschel, Gerald A. Rose, Glenn M. Schaap, and Clayton M. Schooley. The story of the state forest system has been about people as well as trees and lands. There has always been concern within the organization for fellow employees. In the fall of 1966, my wife was diagnosed with a serious and rare condition requiring a long hospital stay. It was very early in my state career, and I didn't have enough sick and vacation time accumulated to cover the anticipated time away from work. We had a three-month-old baby. We lived in Newberry, and the surgery was to be done in Ann Arbor, 350 miles away. My supervisor, Jim Halbach, spoke to regional forester Ernie Hall, who in turn spoke to regional forester R. L. Olmsted in Region III about the situation, unbeknownst to me. Mr. Olmsted called to offer me the opportunity to work at the Ann Arbor office, which happened to be vacant at the time. I could work whatever hours I had available. We were in Ann Arbor for a month, and I was able to work enough hours to stay on the payroll the whole time. It was a wonderful expression of concern for employees—unexpected and undeserved—but greatly appreciated.

Mike Moore especially thanks the many foresters and professionals with whom he has worked over the years. Their friendship, guidance, and leadership have contributed to my career in many different ways. Immediate supervisors Robert A. Borak, Harold Kollmeyer, Weldon J. Montgomery, Roger Rasmussen, Glenn M. Schaap, Henry H. Webster, and those that have passed on (including Ronald Auble, Louis Miller, R. Les Olmstead, and Henry Peterson) were all greatly supportive, each in his own way. When a person has a lifelong career that allows one to look forward to going to work each day, he is truly blessed. Such was my situation in the thirty-seven years that I worked for the department, whether in Lansing, Newberry, Iron Mountain, Cassopolis, St. Charles, Traverse City, Roscommon, or Dimondale. It was great fun and a wonderful place to work.

The authors want to thank members of the MSU Press Staff: Assistant Director and Editor in Chief Julie L. Loehr and Acquisitions Editor Martha A. Bates for their guidance and assistance. We are especially grateful to

Production Manager Annette K. Tanner and Project Editor Kristine M. Blakeslee for their cooperative and helpful attitude and for their dedication and commitment in making this project a success and a reality. The sharp eyes and keen memory of copyeditor Ellen D. Goldlust-Gingrich make the text much easier to read.

Finally, we thank our wives and helpmates, Alice Botti and Drew Moore. Their patience, support, understanding, kindness, and love have made life a joy for more than forty years.

Preface

SURPRISINGLY, NO ONE HAS EVER CHRONICLED THE HISTORY OF MICHIgan's state-owned forests. The detailed events surrounding the development of Michigan's state forest management system represent a fascinating array of actions, dates, facts, and figures regarding the loving care given to public lands by generations of foresters, biologists, technicians, legislators, and others who cared deeply about Michigan's land and its people.

In his book *Forest Sustainability*, Donald W. Floyd notes, "The things that people want from their forests change over time. This challenges our concept of sustainability and our prospects for achieving it. In the past 5,000 years forests have been a place for worship, a source of fuel and fiber, a reservoir for biodiversity, and an important contributor to global climate processes. It is difficult to predict the things that future generations will want from their forests."[1]

Michigan's forests clearly have been many things to many people. We can learn from the past, from our predecessors, who molded largely abandoned, depleted, cutover wastelands into the prosperous, thriving state forests of today. Nearly 4 million acres belong to the citizens of the state producing timber, recreation, wildlife, minerals, water, and mental well-being not only for the ten million residents but also for countless out-of-state visitors.

Timber is certainly part of the story. The raw products that have come off the land in the form of sawlogs, pulpwood, poles, and a huge variety of other categories have fueled industry and provided stability in many northern communities. But many other commodities also characterize Michigan's state forests, including a wide variety of wildlife suitable for hunting, such as black bear, white-tailed deer, and ruffed grouse, as well as species not hunted, such as Kirtland's warbler, porcupines, and bald eagles.

Outdoor recreation—snowmobiling, mushroom picking, fall color tours—comprises a substantial part of the psyche of many Michigan residents. The vast Michigan state forest system provides these and many more opportunities for outdoor recreation. Huge trail networks crisscross the state forests—trails for hiking, cross-country skiing, biking, snowmobiling, off-road vehicles, and horseback riding. Wilderness-style campgrounds abound, and access to lakes, streams, and rivers is almost unfettered.

When we compare the forests of Michigan in 1903 to those of today, the contrast is striking. At that time, the state had practically no forestland; no statewide agency bore responsibility for managing our natural resources; only modest laws protected our resources; forest fires rampaged. Now the top-notch Michigan Department of Natural Resources protects millions of acres using substantial legislation as well as modern fire prevention, detection, and suppression programs. Whereas professional forestry education was in its infancy in 1903, schools of forestry now exist in forty-four states, and Michigan leads the nation with three institutions granting degrees in forestry.

The progress that has occurred over the past hundred years is directly related to the stewardship of the men and women of the organization responsible for forest management on our state-owned lands. Their dedication, service, and commitment have been unsurpassed. The state forests stand as testimony to their unflagging professionalism and dedication.

Foresters have long struggled with the public's tendency to view them as "timber beasts." This view is fostered by the foresters' necessary attention to detail in matters relating to timber and its value. Some might call it a preoccupation, and well it might be in some cases. Foresters take this aspect of their job very seriously.

Looking at it from a different perspective, when we entrust the care of a personal item to someone else, we expect the trustee to take care of the item and protect its value. So it is with our public forests—they are entrusted to the care of the foresters, and we should expect them to be kept in good health and to continue to increase in value and usefulness.

With this book we have attempted to outline the development of the state forest system and to explain some of the thinking that has gone into management decisions along the way. Most of it is based on research of government records and documents, and much of the information in the later chapters is based on our own personal knowledge and experience. We have tried to be objective; if too much feeling and opinion has crept in, we apologize. Our thirty-plus years in the system were wonderful years, full of satisfying accomplishments and lasting friendships. The writing has been a labor of love; we regret we could not include all the tales from our many experiences. Perhaps they will be a topic for a later effort.

We take great pride in the work that has been done on and in our state forests and in the work that has continued since we left state employment. Although we may not be fully aware of what citizens will want from our forests in the future, we do know that the forests are healthy, thriving, and ready to provide whatever is required.

Introduction

AROUND TWELVE THOUSAND YEARS AGO, MELTING GLACIERS IN WHAT IS now the Great Lakes region dropped their accumulated load of rocks, pebbles, boulders, and soil. They left jumbled soils as material of different size and weight washed out of the melting ice and settled in different places. The landscape looked more like a gravel bank than virgin forest. Sand dunes, moraines, drumlins, eskers, and outwash plains formed the landscape that was to support the forests of what eventually became Michigan.

Most of the area rested under glacial Lake Algonquin for about a thousand years before conditions became right for terrestrial plants. Forest establishment likely started about eleven thousand years ago, with aspens, spruces, and other light-seeded species borne on southerly winds. Over the next several hundred years, forests gradually took shape. Fossil pollen studies show that all species did not arrive at once. For example, hemlock, now a common associate of white pine, lagged behind that species by some three thousand years. Moving northward at a rate slower than that of most other species, American chestnut had moved only into the southeast corner of Michigan before chestnut blight struck in the early twentieth century. Perhaps it would have become a component of the northern hardwoods community in another thousand years or so.

Great Lakes scuba divers report the existence of former forests on the bottom of the lakes—not just logs, but entire forests. This finding testifies to changing water levels in response to changing drainage patterns for the northern part of the North American continent. Carbon dating has shown that three thousand years ago, Great Lakes levels were fifty feet or more lower than at present.

Thus, the forests of what is now Michigan have been changing since the glaciers receded. These changes have been wrought by plants' natural tendency to follow predictable patterns of succession from one community type to another in response to various disturbances. Plant communities will respond regardless of the cause of the disturbance.

Fire was a dominant force in shaping the prehistoric forest. Some fires were caused by lightning, and some almost certainly were caused by native peoples as a way of preparing land for agriculture, driving game, or reducing insects or merely by accident. Fires prepared areas for colonization by sun-loving species such as aspens, pines, and oaks.

The primeval forest that greeted European explorers and settlers was shaped by disturbances both large and small, natural and man-made. The forest encountered by LaSalle, Brule, Joliet, Cadillac, and other seventeenth-century explorers was not the same as that which covered the land two hundred years later when settlement by Europeans began in earnest. Tree rings in the old-growth pine at Hartwick Pines State Park have placed the origin of that stand somewhere in the seventeenth century. The pine forests that brought fame to Michigan in 1880 were nothing but brush when LaSalle saw them in 1680.

Michigan's nineteenth-century white pine stands were some of the world's finest. Dense, parklike stands more than 150 feet tall covered vast areas from the Bay City–Muskegon line north. Many prospective settlers saw this as an indication of a highly productive soil that would support agriculture after the pine was removed, a belief that proved true in much of the

Saginaw Valley, where lands are still being farmed more than a century later. Unfortunately, such was not the case in much of northern Michigan.

The vast quantities of timber lured many adventurous and enterprising settlers to Michigan. Lumber became the mainstay of Michigan's economy as residents became adept at harvesting, transporting, and processing pine logs. As Robert Wells shows in his history of the pine era, *Daylight in the Swamp,* some early Michiganders believed that the pine was practically limitless, and would continue to supply the nation for generations to come.[1] Furthermore, residents believed, as the forests were logged, much good timber would grow up in their place, thereby sustaining the industry. In addition to the timber, an active agriculture industry was developing in some places in the wake of the logging. Michigan's economic future based on forest and land resources appeared to be bright. Prosperity was evidently there for the taking, and the taking began in earnest around 1860. Gifford Pinchot, architect of the nation's first forest management policies under President Theodore Roosevelt, remembered how in 1876, "my father took me to the Centennial Exposition at Philadelphia held to celebrate the hundredth birthday of the richest forest country on earth. It contained no forest exhibit of any sort or kind except from the single state of Michigan."[2]

Perhaps the first indication that events were not following the popular plan occurred in 1871. During the first week of October, Michigan settlers experienced fires unlike any they had ever seen. Following two months of serious drought, much of northern Lower Michigan erupted in flames as dry winds fanned the many small fires set as part of land-clearing operations into one unbelievable conflagration. Flames swept across the width of the Lower Peninsula from Lake Michigan to Lake Huron. Many towns, including Holland, Glen Haven, Huron City, Sand Beach, White Rock, and Forestville, were reduced to ashes, while many others suffered significant but not total destruction. The heavy smoke interrupted navigation on Lake Huron and as far downriver as Detroit. More than two hundred people lost their lives; the toll undoubtedly would have been much higher if the area had been more densely populated—the Great Chicago Fire and the infamous Peshtigo Fire in northern Wisconsin occurred at the same time and took an estimated fifteen hundred lives.

Ten years later, in September 1881, a catastrophic fire occurred in the Lower Peninsula area known as the Thumb. Once again, land-clearing fires were whipped together into an inferno at the end of a very dry summer, and once again farms and towns were destroyed with many injuries and much loss of life. Richmondville, Deckerville, Tyne, Bad Axe, Verona Mills, Elk Creek, and Forestville (again) were listed among those towns burned. Where they could, residents fled into lakes and rivers. Some people sought refuge in wells and root cellars. With homes and crops destroyed, the survivors were in a desperate situation. These fires received local and national attention, mostly because of the loss of human life and the destruction of towns and homes. Nearly another decade would pass before people realized that fires were slowly and steadily robbing them of their future forests as well.

As Michigan welcomed more settlers, awareness grew regarding the need to protect, manage, and wisely use the state's natural resources. Yet Michigan continued to think primarily of harvesting rather than conserving its forests.

1

The Awakening

1888–1903

THE YEAR 1888 DAWNED WITH NEW HOPE FOR PROPONENTS OF CONSER-
vation of Michigan's forests. The newly formed State Forestry Commission
invited forestry proponents to a convention in Grand Rapids on January
26–27. An air of optimism prevailed in spite of repeated references to current wasteful practices that constituted a national disgrace.[1]

Keynote speaker Norman A. Beecher, a state representative from Gene-
see County, described the new legislation calling for creation of an Independent Forestry Commission. He said that Michigan could conserve its
forest wealth if only "¼ to ⅓ of its timber is allowed to grow." He cited one
thousand mills and thirty-five thousand jobs along with improving markets
for low-quality wood as evidence of the economic importance of the
forests. Still, unless changes were made, Beecher predicted that Michigan's
timber would not last longer than fifteen years because of the pace of the
cutting and the practices being used.[2]

Other speakers encouraged the planting of trees on barren parts of farms, urged fire prevention, and noted the potential profits from managing timber and from water conservation. At least two speakers referred to the effects of forest removal on the local hydrology, lamenting the lack of data on forests' effects on climate.[3] All in all, the forestry convention seemed a fitting way to begin a new era of forest stewardship and conservation.

One of those attending the convention who led the battle to stem the progressive loss of forests was Dr. William James Beal (1833–1924). Beal, a Harvard graduate, was a man of many talents. He was a professor of botany at State Agricultural College (now Michigan State University) from 1870 to 1910 and held the title professor of forestry from 1883 to 1896. By his own count, he authored more than twelve hundred publications. Beal had a long-standing love of trees and repeatedly voiced concerns regarding the future of Michigan's forests in the face of the exploitation that was taking place in the north. In the early 1870s, he established a campus arboretum by planting 150 species of trees and shrubs along Michigan Avenue. In 1896 he established the Beal Pinetum, one of the oldest surviving forestry test plantings in the state. In 1888 he was appointed a director of the newly formed State Forestry Commission.[4]

The Forestry Commission had been created by the Michigan Legislature's passage of Act 259 of the Public Acts of 1887. The commission was comprised of members of the State Board of Agriculture and was to investigate the extent of destructive fires and wasteful cutting or clearing and to recommend legislation to the governor. Township supervisors were responsible for making "a careful estimate of the area and condition as to the stage of growth, density and character of forest land," including areas suitable for planting. The supervisors were to file annual reports on areas burned in fires over an acre in size and on timber, buildings, fences, and other property destroyed.

Beal initiated other projects to further the cause. In 1888 he established test plantings at Au Sable, Baldwin, Grayling, Harrison, and Walton in northern Lower Michigan to demonstrate the feasibility of reforestation and determine which species would be best suited to this pursuit.[5] Of the five, the Grayling site is by far the best preserved. It was part of the agriculture experiment station and included three levels of site preparation: (1) total cultivation, (2) disking only, and (3) nothing beyond timber harvest. Of the more than forty species of trees planted, three emerged as the clear choices for reforestation on that site—Norway spruce, red pine, and eastern white pine. Survival and growth were quite good on the cultivated site, quite poor on the disked site, and dismal on the untreated site.

Forestry was promoted at various farmers' institutes held around the state. At an 1889 institute in Big Rapids, Beal talked on sugar bush management and farm woodlot management.[6] He recommended that farmers keep a wooded area at the back of their farms, adjoining woodland similarly reserved by neighboring farmers. Farm woodlands would thus constitute fairly large areas and provide good wildlife habitat and watershed protection. Even today, most farm woodlots conform to this recommendation, although whether this phenomenon indicates the popularity of Beal's ideas is unknown.

In an essay published as part of the Agriculture Report for 1893, Beal outlined the state of forestry in Michigan. The numerous problems facing the advancement of forestry included the lack of knowledgeable people; the selfishness of most people; the lack of paying positions in forestry; the fact that lectures at farmers' institutes were not taken seriously; and the fact that elective college courses (such as forestry) were expensive to offer. In acknowledging these obstacles, Beal observed that "the government ownership and control of much of the forests in the old country gave them a great advantage over our newer country where 'private enterprise' accomplishes almost everything." Commenting on the current approach in Michigan, Beal continued, "Something may be done by forest commissions, but too much is likely to be expected of them, and, to save expenses, somebody will advocate their abolition—and somebody will sooner or later usually succeed."[7]

Those interested in forestry were in the minority. When the township supervisors tendered their reports to the Forestry Commission at the end of 1888, the vast majority of those reporting saw no reason for additional legislation except for perhaps some fire controls as requested by a couple of respondents.[8]

The legislature provided no operational funds for the commission after 1888 and in 1892 repealed the act that had formed it.[9] The Forestry Commission was dead. What or who killed it? The economic depression of the 1890s probably led to a tight revenue situation that may have in turn resulted in the abolition of all "unnecessary expenses." But if people had really cared about forestry, the commission's minimal expenses would hardly have seemed "unnecessary."

THE EXPLOITATION OF TIMBER CONTINUED APACE. THE PEAK OF THE harvest was reached in 1890, with an estimated cut of 4.25 billion board feet.[10] With trees disappearing at such a rate, the chances of saving any significant portion of the pine resource were rapidly dwindling. Some forestry supporters believed that the pine was a lost cause and held onto some hope of saving a portion of the hardwood stands from destruction. Action was needed to save anything at all.

Even though the legislature had killed the Forestry Commission in 1892, several individuals continued to back the idea of a system of publicly owned forests. In his January 7, 1897, message to the legislature, Governor John T. Rich pointed out that "much of the land from which the timber has been stripped is of little value for cultivation." He continued, "A modest appropriation looking to some plan for finally establishing a forestry department of the State is well worthy of your earnest consideration."[11]

In 1898 Professor Volney Spalding of the University of Michigan addressed the Michigan Academy of Sciences, calling for a program of reforestation. Shortly thereafter, Spalding and Charles W. Garfield, who had served on the State Board of Agriculture for the previous twelve years, called a meeting of a joint committee chosen by the university's Board of Regents and the State Board of Agriculture to resume the forestry initiative begun a decade earlier by the Forestry Commission. The meeting was held at the Lansing office of the state land commissioner, and Spalding was elected chairman of the ad hoc group and I. H. Butterfield, secretary of the State Agricultural Society and "a lover of trees and a public-spirited citizen," became the secretary of the new group as well.[12]

Born in Wisconsin in 1848, Garfield had moved to Grand Rapids at the age of ten. He began teaching school at seventeen and graduated from State Agricultural College in 1870. He ran his own nursery business and was a member of the Horticulture Department at State Agricultural College from 1874 to 1878. For four years he conducted the Farm Department at the *Detroit Free Press*. He served as the first president and subsequently as secretary of the State Horticultural Society. He was elected to the state legislature in 1881 and offered the joint resolution that led to the recognition of Arbor Day in Michigan. He was no newcomer to the idea of managing forests. In summing up Michigan's forest situation in the early twentieth century, Garfield cited three recent invasions of the forest, by farmers, loggers, and fires: "In Michigan there stood originally about 300 billion feet of White Pine. Up to 1897 there had been cut in the history of this state only 165 billion feet; yet there is practically none today. What became of the rest of that magnificent white pine? It disappeared, and for it there was nothing to pay—nothing but shame and desolation and future want."[13]

The self-constituted commission met several times and drew up a bill for the state legislature that would formally reestablish the Forestry Commission. Senator Robert D. Graham of Grand Rapids, chair of the Committee on Agricultural Interests, introduced this measure, Senate Bill 441 of 1899. The bill passed, and on June 7, 1899, Governor H. S. Pingree signed Act 227, again making forestry a state-empowered program. In 1900, Garfield became the new commission's president.

The legislation directed the commission to recommend to the commissioner of the State Land Office the withdrawal from sale of two hundred thousand acres of land belonging to the state. The state had acquired these lands either via federal grants during the 1800s or through tax delinquency. Special attention was given to lands in Roscommon and Crawford Counties because they included the headwaters of three major Michigan rivers—the Muskegon, the Manistee, and the Au Sable.[14] The commission began to pursue a plan for state-owned lands, instructing the commissioner of the State Land Office to prepare maps showing "solid bodies" of land to be placed in reservations. In accordance with the Forestry Commission's recommendations, the commissioner of the Land Office withdrew from sale and homestead entry various lands in the west half of Roscommon County and in south-central Crawford County. Commissioners agreed to learn all they could about forestry through reading appropriate journals and contacts with other governmental agencies and people in the forest industry.[15]

In its first *Annual Report*, issued in 1900, the commission stated that it had "no idea of recommending that the State go into forestry upon lands that are valuable for agricultural purposes; but from its investigation, it is satisfied that immense tracts of non-agricultural land exist in the State which can be used in the growth of forests, and which, if managed in a business way, will in time return to the State a good interest upon the investment necessary for their care, and incidentally will add largely to the value of the State by affecting favorably its agriculture, its horticulture and its commerce."[16] Concern for the welfare of the forests of Michigan was becoming evident, but the feeling was far from unanimous.

Some residents of the Grayling and Roscommon areas held no love for the forestry advocates and their "forestry scheme." These naysayers would rather have seen the land developed for what they deemed the higher use of agriculture and feared that the forestry designation would cast their county in an unfavorable light for prospective settlers. Others were miffed at having lost the opportunity to acquire the state lands to strip them of what second-growth timber had developed since the first logging. Letters appeared in the local newspapers urging residents to go to Lansing to tell their representatives that the former forestland should be converted to farms. Charles L. DeWaele, the Roscommon County prosecuting attorney, wrote to the *Crawford County Avalanche* in August 1902, predicting disaster from the practice of forestry: "Farmers . . . will be forced to sell out and vacate their beloved homes. Schools will be closed for lack of funds to maintain them and the Christian religion will be banished and churches demolished; forestry lands will not be taxed and will be taken off the assessment rolls; there will not be enough taxable lands left to keep up county, township and school organizations." Furthermore, he warned, Roscommon residents "will defend our homes against the merciless intruder by all legal means, if possible, and by forcible means if necessary. Citizens of Northern Michigan, let our rallying cry be: 'Down with Forestry!'"[17]

OTHER GROUPS ALSO HAD COMPETING INTERESTS IN THE CUTOVER forestland. Landholding companies from Chicago, Minnesota, Iowa, and Ohio began purchasing large blocks of this land for resale to individual farmers.[18] The companies bought nearly worthless land and resold it in smaller units to immigrant farmers at great profit.[19] The commission's 1901 *Annual Report* observed, "There is a growing conviction among the people who have been most thoughtful about the future of our State, that the method which has been pursued of inducing people to go on poor lands simply because they are cheap, is a mistaken one as a matter of State policy, and an injustice to immigrants."[20] Such profiteering may well have contributed to the resistance to forestry.

Opposition notwithstanding, advocates of forestry pressed on for a reservation of state lands for forestry purposes. Land commissioner Edwin A. Wildey said early in 1902 that the state should not dispose of another acre of public domain for thirty years. Land typically sold for the value of the timber alone: since "the State cannot get a cent more for the lands now than the timber is worth," and since "when denuded the lands are invariably forfeited to the State for non-payment of taxes," Wildey reasoned, the state might as well "save the cost of obtaining tax decrees against the lands and at the same time retain possession of them in case they should prove valuable in the future."[21]

The same year, a bill introduced in the legislature would have deeded most tax-reverted lands to the Forestry Commission. In a report to the commission, George P. Sudworth of the U.S. Bureau of Forestry described the bill and its fate: "This bill was remarkably careful and excellent and was approved by some of the best authorities in the country. Nonetheless, it stirred up great opposition (from (1) Farmers' Granges, (2) Country Editors, and (3) Auditors and Land Office). This opposition was misinformed, but powerful, and the bill failed to pass. The commission came off with an absurdly inadequate appropriation and 60,000 acres of State Forest Reserve." Sudworth encouraged the commission to continue to press for greater land acquisition, arguing that waiting to demonstrate results on the 60,000 acres would take too long and that people would lose interest. "Now is the time to acquire land when there is so much of it from which compact forest reserves may be formed," he advised.[22]

While the Forestry Commission was far from satisfied with the amount of land placed under its control, it began to set up a program for management of the new reserves. The commission hired Maxim Pion of Big Rapids as fire warden from July through October 1902, paying him a salary of one hundred dollars per month.[23] Beal was engaged to make exhibits for fairs across the state.[24]

In addition, the commission hosted a meeting of the American Forestry Association in Lansing on August 27–28, 1902, followed by a field trip to the forest reserve. The meeting drew to Michigan nationally prominent forestry advocates, including John Gifford of New York, the first American to obtain a doctorate in forestry; Thomas Sherrard of the National Forestry Bureau in Washington, D.C.; Otto J. Luebkert, secretary of the American Forestry Association; and Professor Burton Edward Livingston of the University of Chicago. The field trip excursion went by train from Lansing to Bay City to Roscommon and then "by teams" to Higgins Lake. While on the field trip, the travelers were entertained at dinner by forestry commissioner Arthur Hill and his wife, with after-dinner remarks by William Gwinn Mather of the Cleveland-Cliffs Iron Company, Beal, and commissioners Hill and Garfield. All expressed optimism for the success of reforestation.[25]

Not by coincidence, the field trip coincided with a demonstration of the Roscommon area's agricultural potential as well as a flurry of anti-forestry letters to local newspapers, as local residents sought to make clear their opposition to the idea of growing trees on the tax-reverted lands. Reported one newspaper,

> The state forestry commission, with about 30 or more visitors, reached Roscommon on Friday noon. Flags were at half mast on the flagpoles in the village and the reception they received from the people, although civil and without any hostile demonstration, was speakingly that their presence here was not wanted. They were told in unmistakable terms that their forestry scheme cannot and will not be tolerated in the county. Circulars were handed them to that effect. At the Post Office the finest exhibition of cereals, fruits, etc., all raised on farms in the county, and which exhibition they unwillingly were obliged to visit, must have convinced them that Roscommon county is not a barren wilderness, unfit for cultivation, but a county destined to become a great agricultural center.
>
> Their stay at the village was therefore of short duration. They left for the north, with a "God speed and never come back" as a greeting from our people.[26]

Nevertheless, the commission persisted. Having learned from past mistakes, however, the commission attempted to win the support of the people of Roscommon and Crawford Counties before having a bill introduced in the legislature. In 1903, about twenty residents of those northern counties traveled to Lansing for two days of meetings with Garfield, Filibert Roth of the U.S. Bureau of Forestry, Beal, Professor Ernest E. Bogue of Michigan Agricultural College, and Wildey. The commission recommended certain survey townships as the basis for the Forestry Reserve, while the citizens committee countered with their own proposal. According to the minutes of the meeting, "The Commission, after deliberation, accepted the proposition, and the joint committee of the House and Senate were so notified, and a bill was drawn in accordance with their joint action, both parties pledging themselves to do their utmost to carry out the contract."[27] The legislature acted, and Governor Aaron T. Bliss signed Act 175 of 1903 establishing a thirty-four-thousand-acre forestry reserve in Roscommon and Crawford Counties.

2

The Foundation

1903–1907

THE MICHIGAN LEGISLATURE HAD NOW ENDORSED THE CONCEPT OF A system of publicly owned forests. Now, where was the Forestry Commission to start?

The commission members had some firm ideas. On July 16, 1903, they hired Homer Rutledge to serve as fire warden and to survey the land and timber. To get this effort off on the right foot, the commission contacted Gifford Pinchot, a noted conservationist and founder of the U.S. Forest Service who was currently serving as director of the Division of Forestry in the Department of Interior. The commission also sent a delegate to a national forestry convention held on August 25–26 in Minneapolis. In addition, at its July 16 meeting, the commission decided to order five hundred copies of the Forest Reserve Act for public distribution.[1]

On July 27, Pinchot attended a commission meeting in Grand Rapids to support Michigan's forestry effort. He said he liked the look of things in

Filibert Roth, first forest warden for Michigan's state forestlands and first director of the School of Forestry at the University of Michigan. Courtesy of the Bentley Historical Library, University of Michigan.

Michigan but preferred Wisconsin's approach, considering it to be more comprehensive, and he told Michigan's forestry advocates that if the state made a good showing on its initial forest reserves, the legislature would feel obligated to expand the program. Also in attendance at Grand Rapids were C. D. Smith, director of the State Experiment Station, and two professors from the University of Michigan, one of whom was to play a key role in moving the state forward.[2]

Filibert Roth was born in Württemberg, one of Germany's well-known forest areas, on April 20, 1858. In September 1870 his family immigrated to the United States. Young Roth was somehow separated from his parents and ended up in Sauk City, Wisconsin, where he was apprenticed to a shoemaker. At the age of sixteen, he rejoined his father at his ranch near Fort Worth, Texas. Two years later, on June 23, 1876, Filibert found his father murdered and shortly thereafter left for Wyoming and Montana, where he drove cattle, herded sheep, and hunted buffalo. During these adventures, he read what books he could in an effort to compensate for a lack of formal schooling. He returned to Sauk City in 1883, where he taught school and did woodworking in the summers.[3]

Roth entered the University of Michigan in 1885 and received his bachelor of science degree in 1890. He then spent three years doing graduate work in botany, zoology, and geology, including courses in forestry taught by Professor Volney Spaulding. Roth then went to work for Dr. B. E. Fernow in the federal Bureau of Forestry, remaining there until 1898, when Roth, Fernow, and Dr. John C. Gifford left to form the faculty of the New York State College of Forestry at Cornell. In 1901, Cornell's school of forestry was dissolved, and Roth returned to work for the Bureau of Forestry, where he became administrator of the National Forest Reserves under Pinchot's supervision.

At the time of the July 1903 meeting in Grand Rapids, Roth had already agreed to move to the University of Michigan to organize and head its Department of Forestry. He was well known in Michigan and had highly valuable federal experience in management of the public lands. Thus, it seemed natural to put Roth in charge of the new state forest reserves. Pinchot agreed to allow Roth to work in that capacity until he assumed his duties at the university, and the university agreed to allow him time to perform those duties after he joined the faculty.

Before the meeting ended, Pinchot expressed concern that the existence of two forestry schools in Michigan might cause them to waste valuable energy in competition with one another. His concerns were eased by the explanation that the two schools would divide responsibilities, with Michigan Agricultural College emphasizing farm forestry and the University of Michigan doing postgraduate work. Pinchot stressed that people needed to know that cutover lands could produce timber again. At the close of the meeting, the secretary of the Forestry Commission, Edwin A. Wildey, recorded "a very general awakening to the importance of reforestation in Michigan." Moreover, he continued, "The meeting held this week perhaps marks the beginning of an important epoch which shall add greatly to the value of Michigan forest cover."[4]

EFFECTIVE SEPTEMBER 17, ROTH BECAME FOREST WARDEN, WITH THE Forestry Commission paying the University of Michigan one thousand dollars per year for his services. Roth thus effectively became Michigan's first state forester. He was instructed to proceed with investigations of the lands dedicated as the Forest Reserves. Just over a week later, Roth reported that nine thousand acres had been reviewed in the South Reserve in ten-acre sections and that "corners of sections had been established for 25 miles." The commission authorized him to negotiate for additional lands, give free permits for wild hay to local farmers, dispose of dead and down timber (valued under ten dollars and for domestic use), and employ William S. Emery of Roscommon County as forest ranger at a salary of five hundred dollars per year plus expenses when on special detail. His work was to be at the still-to-be-established nursery, establishing property corners, and performing other needed work. Emery's other duties included the construction of fire lines, the first systematic fire-control effort on wild lands in Michigan.[5]

The construction of a seedling nursery to aid in reforestation received a great deal of attention in the early days of Roth's tenure as forest warden. In December 1903, Roth expressed his thanks in advance to Pinchot for "plans for formation of Forestry nurseries on the Michigan State Forestry reserve near Roscommon, Mich." and received authority from the commission to "purchase such seeds and seedlings as he may deem necessary to carry out the plan for the seed beds and plants." The commission also approved purchase of other materials needed for the nursery.[6]

The best of intentions somehow came to naught, however, and in February 1904, Roth announced that the U.S. Bureau of Forestry was unable to provide the promised assistance with nursery plans. The warden took on this project to go with his many other concerns.[7] Among other things, he needed a more definite strategy for management of the reserves, and he needed more manpower. Roth developed a detailed plan of action for 1904, which he submitted to the commission at the February meeting. Roth proposed the retention of the ranger at the North Reserve as well as the addition of a similar position at the South Reserve. Moreover, he suggested that a second ranger be added at the North Reserve and that the two men's duties be expanded to include the establishment of the nursery. He estimated a 1903–4 budget for all these activities of $3,573.[8] The Forestry Commission approved the forester position for the northern reserve, and Wesley Bradfield was added to the payroll in April, but other parts of the plan stubbornly refused to materialize.[9]

One problem was the survey of land conditions, an effort that involved attempting to get a reasonably accurate picture of what species of trees were on the land as well as their size, form, general health, age, and spacing. In addition, information on the soil type, ground cover, land form, access roads, and survey lines was needed. And as Forestry Commission President Charles W. Garfield wrote in February 1904, "We are anxious to do the work in such a way that it need not be repeated, and that plantations, fire lines and timber sales can readily be planned from the data obtained."[10]

Examination of the forest reserve land proceeded with student help from the University of Michigan. The resulting 1904 report described a typical acre as having 100 pine stumps; 160 oak "stools" or sprout clumps; 75 small, bushy jack pines; and 80 percent of the ground covered by sweet ferns. Most of the land had been burned several times. White pine seedlings were often present, but the frequent fires prevented their advance to sapling size. The report also noted numerous existing uses of the state lands in the reserves, most notably picking blueberries, which thrived after fires. Cattle grazing use was considerable, especially in the northern district, where controls had become necessary; however, Roth believed that the benefit from grazing outweighed the negative effects on forest development. Reserve lands were heavily hunted in deer season, although "little remains to kill." There were many hunting accidents, and some fires were attributed to hunters, but this contention was never verified.[11]

Each district had a forest ranger that patrolled against fires and trespass to beneficial effect. Rangers wore a badge with the wording "Forest Reserve Ranger" encircling a large letter "M."[12]

Roth made progress on other fronts as well. He established a nursery north of Higgins Lake in Roscommon County, in 1903 . In the process of

◯ PLAN OF MANAGEMENT OF THE ROSCOMMON FOREST RESERVE, 1904

The following preliminary plan for the management of the Roscommon forest reserves was respectfully submitted by Warden Roth and adopted.

A. Roscommon Reserve South.

   1. For administration and protection. One forest ranger is retained throughout the year at present compensation and duties.

   2. The work of the year will consist in:

      a. Protection of reserve; fire and trespass

      b. Preparation of ground for seed beds to be used in spring, 1905

      c. Survey of lands, to be continued either and preferably under co-operation with Bureau of Forestry, or else to be carried on piecemeal by permanent reserve force.

      d. Establishment of permanent headquarters, at or near seed-bed grounds.

      e. Attention to cases of free use of hay and wood, cases of grazing, and sale of timber.

      f. Special examination of lands in cases where such lands are offered for sale or exchange.

B. Roscommon Reserve North.

   1. For administration and protection. One forester at rate of $720.00 per year, and one ranger at rate of $500.00 per year, both to be retained throughout the year.

   2. The work of the year to consist of:

      a. Protecting of the reserve, especially of seed beds and plantations.

      b. Establishment of seed bed and care of same, at nursery in Sec. 36, T.25N., R.4W.

      c. Planting of 50,000 young trees on denuded land of SE 1/4, Sec 36, T.25N., R.4W.

---

getting the nursery up and running, the warden and his staff did battle continuously with gophers, mice, birds, and an infestation of weeds. Of particular concern was the trailing dewberry, which seemed impossible to eradicate. Roth also established a headquarters on newly acquired land adjacent to the nursery, although, he reported, "the buildings are inadequate, consisting of a one-room log hovel and a small barn with a mere semblance of a roof."[13]

d. Preparation of ground for seed bed, to be seeded in 1905.

e. Establishment of ranger headquarters.

f. Survey of lands, to be carried on incidentally to other work. This work to be done by Forester (both here and in Roscommon Reserve South) with assistance of Rangers and volunteer assistance of students.

ESTIMATE OF EXPENSES

For the Fiscal Year 1903–1904.

Salary of Warden, Sept. 16, 1903, to June 30, 1904 . . . . $788.

Salary of Ranger for Roscommon Reserve South.

    October 1, 1903, to June 30, 1904. . . . . $375.

Expenses of Survey, August and September, 1903, ... $370.

Equipment to February 29, 1904, ... $109.

Team of horses and wagon, ... $300.

Feed, 2½ months, ... $ 60.

Camp equipment, tents, tools, plow, harrow, nails, etc. . . . . $250.

Seeds for seed-beds, ... $ 90.

Lumber for 700 beds, ... $360.

Plants (young trees) 50,000 . . . . $250.

Salary for Ranger, Roscommon Reserve North, at rate of $500.00 per year,

    April 1, to June 30, 1904 . . . . $105.

Salary, Forester, April 15, to June 30, 1904 at rate of $720.00 per year

    (of 365 days) . . . . $225.

Extra help in planting, seed bed work, etc. . . . . $150.

Traveling expenses and other incidentals, express, etc. . . . . $ 50.

Contingent fund for fire, ... $100.

. . . . $3573.

The first state forest planting occurred in the spring of 1904 on Lot 8, Section 36, Township 25 North, Range 4 West, using purchased seedlings. The trees planted included thirty thousand white pine, ten thousand Norway spruce, ten thousand Scotch pine, and one thousand black locust. Local laborers planted the trees, and for those men, Roth observed, the idea of doing something other than destruction in the forest was a new one. However, he noted, "The same men who began their planting work with doubtful glance and sneer in their speech went away converted, the work had produced a large part of the change from the mere wood butcher into the forester, the man who is interested as much in seeing a tree start and grow as he is in the cutting of timber and its conversion."[14]

His 1904 report closed on another positive note. "There should also be mentioned here the complete change in the attitude of the people of both Roscommon and Crawford counties, not only with regard to the Reserves but also with regard to forestry in general. The opposition, due in a large measure to a misunderstanding of the real objectives of the Reserves, and undoubtedly stimulated and irritated by misrepresentations of interested persons has passed away almost entirely."[15]

DESPITE THE SHORTAGE OF LABOR AND FUNDING, THE MANAGEMENT OF the reserves proceeded to work on the three major concerns: fire control, re-forestation, and trespass (both in the sense of timber trespass [the cutting of timber from land belonging to another] and in the sense of building trespass [the construction of buildings on land owned by another]). The commission also tackled such other concerns as grazing, whether the reserves should pay property tax, whether excess nursery stock should be sold to the public, whether the commission should sell Christmas trees from the reserves, whether the state should allow portable sawmills and the cutting of dead timber, and what should be done about the sunken logs in Wolf Creek and Boise Lake. In almost all cases, the commission deferred to Roth to resolve these issues, and many of the policies instituted at that time have continued until the present.

At the September 1908 Forestry Commission meeting, for example, Roth described a building trespass discovered during the land survey. Should the offender be forced to remove the buildings? At the suggestion of commissioner William Mershon, the trespasser traded a tract of land for the tract on which he had constructed the buildings.[16]

In 1903, the Michigan Legislature had passed Act 249, which provided for a system of forest fire wardens, prohibited various actions that could contribute to forest fires, and prescribed fines for violations. The legislature failed to provide funding for enforcement of the act, however, and it therefore was largely ineffective. Four years later, the legislature passed Act 106, which reorganized the effort by transferring responsibility for enforcing the antifire measures to the state game, fish, and forestry warden.[17] Nevertheless, the presence of fire wardens with authority to impress labor and enforce laws did not alleviate the need for special fire control efforts on the forest reserves. A system of fire lines was constructed in the forest reserves by clearing brush and stumps down to bare mineral soil in lines running both east-west and north-south every quarter of a mile. These lines served as access roads and as barriers to surface fires.

The year 1908 was a dry one and saw numerous forest fires, some of them severe. At its September 1908 meeting, the members of the Forestry Commission discussed the subject and asked Roth "whether the fire lanes had been a protection." Although "Roth answered unqualifiedly in the affirmative, . . . he said it was impossible to fight forest fires coming in upon the reserve from the outside and at the same time take care of a hidden enemy within who was constantly adding to the trials of the fire fighters by starting numerous fires within the limits of the reserve." In light of Roth's certainty that someone was deliberately setting these fires, the commission authorized him to investigate the incidents and institute proceedings against anyone who started a fire within the reserves.[18]

As the forest warden's responsibilities expanded, it became increasingly difficult for Roth to balance the demands of that job with those of his primary position as a professor at the University of Michigan. Roth had done an admirable job of getting the forest reserves up and running and of setting a direction for their management, but the commissioners decided that they needed to devise a more efficient long-term plan for managing the reserve, particularly in light of the rampant 1908 fires. On December 14, Garfield wrote to James B. Angell, president of the University of Michigan, that with the forestry reserves' increasing expenses, especially those incurred as a result of the fires, the Forestry Commission could no longer provide a thousand dollars per year to the university for its forestry school.[19] Clouds of smoke had been all too common over the forest reserves, and clouds were forming as well over the management of the state lands.

3

Getting Organized

1907–1909

WHILE THE FORESTRY COMMISSION WAS STRUGGLING WITH FIRES AND finances, another commission was struggling with the practices common on the state lands outside the forest reserves and in the State Land Office. Governor Fred M. Warner appointed a special Commission of Inquiry on Tax Lands and Forestry by authority of Act 188 of 1907. After completing its work, the Commission of Inquiry issued a scathing report on conditions and practices and described an orgy of greed and exploitation.

State lands had been sold for years under the Homestead Act of 1862, which was intended to encourage settlers on the state lands. A purchaser was required to establish a residence and to clear a certain portion of the land for farming. The Commission of Inquiry's investigations turned up information indicating that less than 5 percent of the land sold under the act had been truly settled.[1] The vast majority of the lands had gone to timber companies and speculators.

Some "settlers" built the rudest of shacks to meet the law's requirements; some used buildings left from the pine logging, in various states of
decay, to pass as the required residences. Some made no attempt to comply
with the law but went straight to work stripping timber from the land.
Many such owners never paid any taxes on the land, letting it revert to state
ownership for a second or even third time.[2]

Speculators bought square-mile sections for fifty cents an acre and then
subdivided the land into smaller parcels and sold it to would-be farmers for
what amounted to twelve, fifteen, or even twenty dollars per acre.[3] Some of
the same speculators sold hundreds of resort lots in the Higgins Lake area.
Most of this land soon proved nonproductive and was returned to the state
in lieu of payment of taxes. According to the report, such speculation had
been so common in Roscommon County, for example, "that it is claimed by
the companies themselves that two Chicago land syndicates today control
over two-thirds of the land of the county."[4]

In 1908, the *Grand Rapids Herald* quoted state forest and game warden
Charles S. Pierce as saying,

> It certainly is a great shame that certain companies can buy sand wastes
> from the State at 50 cents an acre and sell at $10 an acre to the poor steel
> workers and others in the large cities that have dreams of the independence
> of the farmer. I notice each week in the Chicago papers great ads, which are
> intended to entice men from the large cities to these barrens, where it is
> pictured that they will be in the land of milk and honey and independent
> for life. A man will have more fun for his money by throwing it into the
> lake and seeing the splash. When these poor fellows from the cities buy a
> section of this land they expect to be able to grow something upon it. The
> result is they eke out a miserable existence for a year or so and then aban-
> don the farm and are glad to get back to the city, where the pay envelope is
> handed out each Saturday night.
>
> There should be some legislation of some sort to prevent this sort
> of speculation. I don't know what would be required but certainly some-
> thing is.

The State Land Office, too, came under intense criticism for its methods of operation. State trespass agents stationed in the field had authority

to impose and collect fines and fees, but months sometimes passed before the money collected was remitted to Lansing.[5] Moreover, these agents had great leeway in applying the law: some poor families were fined for cutting a few trees to build a home and forced to mortgage their farms to pay the fines, while other trespassers received mere slaps on the wrist. For example, one man illegally cut 250,000 board feet of pine from state land, with a value of several thousand dollars, yet paid the state only a total of $16.95. In the same area, a poor farmer was fined $30 for cutting timbers to build a house. The report also cited instances in which state agents had issued fines for trespass on lands to which the state did not hold title.[6]

The investigators whose work formed the backbone of the report cataloged numerous other abuses of the system. In some cases, they said, "it seems doubtful if the appraiser ever actually visited the land." In other instances, "The appraising is poorly done, without instructions as to thoroughness, without control, and consequently leaves the State office entirely without any knowledge worth the name. In addition the lack of inspection and control makes it possible for interested persons to direct, influence and modify this appraisal for their own benefit."[7] Cheboygan County was named as the site of many suspicious and peculiar situations: prospective purchasers guided appraisers around and then bought land for less than its true value—as little as one to two dollars per acre.[8] In one case, an owner had failed to pay taxes for fifteen or sixteen years. When an appraiser came to begin the process of repossessing the land, the "owner" guided the official around the property and then bought the parcels he wanted for $1.25 per acre, far less than the actual value of $6.00 per acre, despite the fact that the tracts contained standing timber worth $2,300. The end result was that the man acquired more than $3,000 worth of property for $200 after having held it tax-free for fifteen years.[9]

In Mecosta County the report described a "reprehensible condition." Lumber companies removed timber, neglected to pay taxes, and sold the land via quitclaim deeds to settlers who failed to understand that such deeds do not necessarily convey clear title. The settlers paid taxes on these lands for as long as twenty years before learning that the previous owners still owed taxes. The settlers often had to mortgage their property to pay those back taxes, but the land was generally not productive enough to cover the extra cost of the mortgage.[10]

The white pine logging era is often viewed as a time of benign neglect when tax laws encouraged timber companies to remove trees from the land and then let it revert to the state. Loggers and lumbermen considered their activities beneficial to society, preparing the way for an agricultural industry that was sure to follow. "The plow will follow the axe," went the common refrain. While this view contained a grain of truth, the report of the Commission of Inquiry shows that much more was taking place. The timber barons had no respect for the land itself but saw it simply as a vehicle for making quick profits.[11] If doing so meant swindling the state and its people, so be it.

A huge amount of land reverted to the state as a result of the owners' failure to pay taxes. Between 1875 and 1905, the area of tax-delinquent land at any one time varied from 5 million to 9 million acres—between 28 percent and 50 percent of the total land area of the northern counties. The exploitation of these lands amounted to big business. Some Upper Peninsula newspapers collected more in advertising revenue related to buying and selling of the state lands than their counties received in tax revenue.[12] And with every instance of exploitation, every failed farming attempt and every wildfire, the productivity of the land further declined. William B. Mershon, a member of the Forestry Commission, commented in 1908, "I spent five days around Harrison and I saw abandoned farms in great numbers. I will bet I saw 100 farm houses boarded up and desolate, and in some of them were the cook stoves, rocking chairs and a lot of other stuff left behind, for they evidently had no money to cart it away. A whole lot of life's tragedy is written on the Michigan sand barrens. New settlers are going in right along to try the same old experiment of threshing a living out of the sand and nothingness, and will meet with the same result."[13] Changes needed to be made quickly to prevent the state from destroying itself.

Having studied the situation, the Commission of Inquiry made a series of recommendations regarding the tax-reverted lands.[14]

1. Good farmland should be identified and reserved for settlers, thereby defusing the argument that the forestry movement was at odds with agriculture.
2. Forest reserves should be secured. The reserves should be large enough to provide for future forest needs but should be limited to

William Mershon (1856–1943) was a descendant of one of Michigan's first lumber barons, E. J. Mershon, who arrived in Saginaw in 1854 from Rochester, New York, and joined with Jesse Hoyt to build the first planing mill in the Saginaw Valley. He became a well-known businessman in the valley, running his mill around the clock and opening a saltworks as well. Later, William Mershon expanded his interests to the western states with timber and copper mining operations. He served for many years on the Michigan Forestry Commission and was very active in the Michigan Forestry Association. He was a great outdoorsman and sportsman and was the author of *The Passenger Pigeon* and *Recollections of My Fifty Years of Hunting and Fishing*. His son attended the Biltmore School at Pisgah, North Carolina, the first school of forestry in the United States.

Mershon spent his later years supervising the construction of the Lumbermen's Monument along the Au Sable River in Iosco County. He died at his home in Saginaw on July 12, 1943.

about 25 percent of any county to provide a proper mix of farms and forests.

3. State lands not needed for either farms or forest reserves should be made available for industrial, municipal, and residential use in such a way that development would not interfere with farming or forestry.

4. Control over damming of streams should be reserved by the state to prevent speculators from building dams to create more water frontage and consequently increase land values.

5. A system of fire control and commercial and farm forestry should be instituted. The report proposed a structure of twenty-five districts, each with a deputy warden at its head and a sufficient number of local fire wardens. Above the deputies would be a forest warden, who would take the place of the current game, fish, and forestry warden and other officials. Subdepartments would oversee various aspects of resource management. All appointments would be on the basis of training and education, not politics.

6. The state should make payments to local governments to offset tax revenues lost to forest reserves.

7. Private forest reserves should be established as a means of educating people in the principles and application of forestry practices in second-growth timber. An owner could gain title to the land after twenty-five years of management in compliance with fire control and other forest management regulations.
8. Natural regeneration should be emphasized wherever possible to counteract the general disregard for young trees.

It was difficult to say just where the forest reserves should be situated, since the land continued to cycle from state to private ownership and back to the state. But the report's message was clear: some means must be found to return the poorer land to productivity, and that productivity must logically take the form of forests.

The report also included other recommendations for the benefit of forestry in general. The most important of these involved measures designed to prevent the destruction of the forests by fire, the main threat. Improvement of the tax structure, organization of a statewide fire protection force and concentration of authority for fire, trespass, game and fish management in state government were the most prominent.

The Commission of Inquiry noted that little attention had been given by the state to the value of natural regeneration on the tax-reverted lands, even though there was ample documentation of their restocking potential in the absence of fire. A section of the commission's report was dedicated to letters documenting the success of natural regeneration from farmers and others across the state. All qualified this success, however, as being dependent on the control of fires. Without fire protection, no amount of fiscal or political reform would accomplish much. Mershon observed in 1908 that fire wardens also served as game wardens and that they were perceived as preferring to do the latter work.[15] Although they had the authority to impress labor to fight fires, the wardens were not required to act. The commission's report recommended the creation of a force of several hundred men—not political appointees—to control fires across northern Michigan.[16]

Finally, the commission recommended a reorganization of state government agencies related to forests and forestry. Current arrangements resulted in a confusing tangle, with overlapping responsibilities among offices and poor performance in protecting the interests of the people. The commission called for formation of a Public Domain Commission to handle the affairs of the public lands, forests, and rural police. The new commission would appoint a forest warden to take the place of the game, fish, and forestry warden and other officials. Subdepartments would handle the various aspects of resource management. The report's authors again noted the importance of appointing qualified persons rather than the politically well-connected to these positions.[17]

The Michigan Legislature concurred with this recommendation, forming the new Public Domain Commission through Act 280 of the Public Acts of 1909. The legislation addressed most of the needs identified by the Commission of Inquiry, and the new commission started afresh, with a totally new slate of officers.

4

Custodial Management

1909–1920

THE PUBLIC DOMAIN COMMISSION TOOK OVER THE MANAGEMENT OF
the state forest reserves on July 1, 1909. The members of the Forestry Commission spent little time during their final meeting discussing the change, and none of the commissioners carried over to the new body. The complete change in personnel could not have been accidental, yet no explanation appears in the record.

Former forest warden Filibert Roth had occasional communication with the new commission regarding bills to be paid and other business.[1] Former forestry commissioner William B. Mershon had more contact with the new governing body, as he defended his right of ownership of a number of seedlings growing in the nursery at the time of the changeover.[2] Mershon also occasionally wrote to the Public Domain Commission to express his opinions. Former Forestry Commission chair Charles W. Garfield wrote to the new commission more than a year after the changeover, offering his

Dr. C. A. Schenck's Biltmore Forestry School class, in what is now the Pisgah-Croatan National Forest in Asheville, North Carolina. Marcus Schaaf, a 1904 graduate of the school, is seated on the log in the center of the photograph. Courtesy of the Forest History Society, Durham, North Carolina.

assistance: "I have just perused the report of Forester Griffiths [*sic*] of Wisconsin. This illustrates in a graphic way what a live forester can do. I trust you have a copy. Michigan, under your Commission, has a better opportunity now than Wisconsin, because your powers are so broad. If the lawmakers will arise to the situation and give you funds, I have great hope. Command me if I can give you a helping hand."[3] Outside of these occasional contacts, however, the Public Domain Commission was on its own.

The new commission had six members: the auditor general, the commissioner of the state land office, the secretary of state, a member of the Board of Regents of the University of Michigan, a member of the State Board of Agriculture, and a member of the Board of Control of the College of Mines at Houghton. The commission also had three staff positions: a secretary, an assistant secretary, and a bookkeeper.[4]

At the second meeting of the Public Domain Commission, held on August 12, 1909, Commissioner William Kelly of Vulcan, who represented the College of Mines, was charged with beginning the process of employing a forester and with communicating "with Mr. Marcus Schaaf of Munising and request[ing] him to be present at the next meeting of the Commission." Schaaf, a graduate of the Biltmore School of Forestry in North Carolina, attended the September 8 meeting and gave remarks on the forest situation in Michigan. Former state senator E. B. Linsley of Three Rivers submitted the name of O. L. Sponsler, a forestry student at the University of Michigan, as another candidate for the forester position. The commission's Executive Committee was charged with considering the matter.[5]

The Public Domain Commission also had to resolve some unfinished Forestry Commission business. The new commission's proceedings noted accounts due from timber cut in 1908, and the commissioners complained that good records had not been kept. The new commission decided not to honor cutting permits that the old Forestry Commission had intended to be active through the year 1910.[6]

Supervisors from Roscommon County invited the commission to send a representative to discuss "an organization for the settlement of vacant lands and a better understanding between State and local authorities along this line."[7] Despite the progress that Roth had noted years earlier, acceptance of forestry in northern Michigan remained slow in coming, and the supervisors remained inclined to promote farming on the cutover lands.

The Michigan Forestry Association, a citizen organization concerned about Michigan's forests, requested that a representative of the Public Domain Commission attend the group's annual meeting in Jackson on November 9. Junius Beal, the commission member from the University of Michigan, attended and subsequently remarked, "Great credit is due the Forestry Association of this State for its arousing public opinion so strongly as to secure the passage of this law under which we are operating. . . . One of their suggestions which appeals to me is the need of a good forester—one who not only knows about woodcraft, but can tell about it interestingly."[8]

At the Public Domain Commission's November meeting, Huntley Russell, commissioner of the State Land Office, was appointed to approach Schaaf to see "if satisfactory arrangements could be made for his employment at [one hundred dollars per month plus expenses] and for not too long a period."⁹ Schaaf's appointment became official on March 10, 1910, and he remained in the position for nearly forty years. He took up residence at Higgins Lake as Michigan's second state forester and began the business of managing the two "state forests."

Almost immediately after Schaaf's hiring, questions began to occur to the commission. "Do we pay taxes on the reserves?" "Who will do the Annual Report? (It needs a report from the Fire Warden and others.)" "Who supervises the State Forester?" "What do we do with the nursery's surplus seedlings?" "Can we deduct operating costs from timber revenue before submitting same to the State treasury?" Augustus C. Carton, secretary to the commission, assumed responsibility for answering these and many other questions.¹⁰

In accordance with the legislation that had created it, the Public Domain Commission assumed the duties of the State Land Office, then headed by Huntley Russell. The Land Office controlled the sale of state lands and oversaw the work of the supervisor of trespass, Glen R. Munshaw, and his field force of trespass officers. The state forester was placed under Russell's supervision.¹¹

The commission also bore responsibility for fire protection on all the state-owned lands. Lands other than the state forests were protected by an organization of fire wardens headed by Charles Pierce, the game, fish, and forestry commissioner. Schaaf was appointed a fire warden so that he could conscript labor as needed to fight fires on the state forests, for which responsibility he received an additional two hundred dollars per year.¹²

Fire-fighting help was also available from the Northern Forest Protective Association, a private concern headed by Thomas B. Wyman of Munising that covered the Upper Peninsula and charged a per-acre fee for service.¹³ The Michigan Hardwood Manufacturers' Association offered similar services in the northern Lower Peninsula. Reports on the effectiveness of these various agencies vary, but the availability of help from private companies testifies to the level of concern regarding fire.

OPENING UP A STATE FOREST FOR MANAGEMENT INVOLVED THE HIRING of a custodian, the selection of a headquarters site, and the erection of necessary buildings. The cost of this operation, including the salary of the

∾ MARCUS SCHAAF

Michigan's longest-serving state forester, Marcus Schaaf, (1880–1959) officially held the position from March 10, 1910, until March 1, 1949, likely the longest tenure of any state forester in U.S. history.

Schaaf was teaching school in Indiana when he read a *Saturday Evening Post* article about the new profession of forestry. After looking into the various schools available, he enrolled in Dr. Carl A. Schenck's Biltmore School of Forestry at Pisgah, North Carolina, graduating in 1904. After spending the next two years working in Arkansas and Wyoming, Schaaf came to Michigan to work for the Cleveland-Cliffs Iron Company at Negaunee, including work on Grand Island in Lake Superior. He remained in this position until he took the job of state forester.

Marcus Schaaf. Courtesy of the Michigan Department of Natural Resources.

Under Schaaf's leadership, Michigan's state forest system grew from thirty-five thousand acres to more than 3.6 million acres, including nearly a quarter of a million acres of planted pine. He pioneered nursery operations and reforestation as well as public forest administration. As a registered surveyor, he was an authority on the reestablishment of the legal corners on state forestland originally established by the federal government in the middle of the nineteenth century.

In the early days, much of his work time was spent in the Higgins Lake area, where he often took his family to a cottage considered the summer headquarters of the state forester. His daughter Miv, a columnist for the *Los Angeles Times*, frequently wrote of her fond memories of those times. She said of his retirement "he was given a gold watch and packed all his books from the cottage while mother emptied the goldenrod from the Mason jar on the table, packed our dishes and took down the old red tin tray from the mantel. We left the toasting forks."

custodian, amounted to between five thousand and six thousand dollars annually.[14] Under Roth's direction, the Forestry Commission had established the Higgins Lake and Houghton Lake forests, and Schaaf picked up where they left off, operating the nursery, constructing fire lines, and salvaging dead and down timber. Schaaf was also assigned to examine other reserve lands and make recommendations for management as well as to devise solutions to the never-ending parade of requests for land exchanges.

In February 1911, Schaaf reported to the commission on his examination of the existing reserves, which he called "State Forests." He described the Fife Lake Reserve, the Forest of Lakes Reserve (located in both Grand Traverse and Kalkaska Counties), and the Luce County Reserve. Of the thirty-five-thousand-acre Luce County tract, he wrote, "We have in this case conditions that cannot be duplicated in any of our State Forests. The lands are pre-eminently suited for forestry purposes. In large measure, it is already fairly well stocked with young growth. There are no railroads, very few inhabitants, and but few people come and go; therefore the chances of fire are greatly reduced. There is at hand ready, with a little labor, to serve as fire lines, a network of old roads and railroad grades extending in all directions. There are practically no conflicting interests, since about eighty-five per cent of the land is controlled by parties who are in full sympathy with forest protection." The tract contained only two decent roads, making access difficult, and most people who came to pick the area's primary crop, blueberries, came by water. Schaaf recommended the building of two ranger cabins and a barn plus two fire towers, with an estimated cost of six thousand dollars.[15]

The Fife Lake State Forest contained about seventy-two hundred acres of state land, mostly in pine land. Schaaf observed that there was little chance of natural reproduction here unless fire lines were built soon along the several railroads that crossed the tract. The Forest of Lakes State Forest consisted of about four thousand acres just west of Kalkaska. Here there was some potential for natural reproduction and some need for planting. Preliminary reports were also made on the Black Lake State Forest, forty-two hundred acres in Cheboygan and Presque Isle Counties, and the Ogemaw State Forest, which consisted of about five thousand acres in Ogemaw County, near West Branch.[16]

In June 1913, Frank Van Sickle was hired as custodian for the Fife Lake forest, and a site was chosen for the headquarters on a lake now known as Headquarters Lake. It was located some twenty miles southeast of Traverse City in the SW ¼ of the SE ¼ of Section 23, Township 25 North, Range 9 West.[17] The Public Domain Commission gave Schaaf authority to open management in Luce County and authorized a budget for the 1913–14 fiscal year. Walter Hatch, who had previously worked in the Higgins Lake forest, was hired as custodian for the Lake Superior State Forest (the Luce County tract) in July 1913.[18] The Ogemaw tract was added in 1914, with the Presque Isle area following in 1915, the Alpena Reserve coming in 1916, and the Pigeon River area added in 1919.

In 1915 the commission took stock of its situation and examined current policies and procedures. That fall, the commissioners drafted a formal policy for the state forests, including work priorities for the coming years. Many of the state's major forest advocates, including Garfield and Roth, convened in Lansing to discuss the draft policy and procedures. Some amount of fence-mending apparently took place, and the former forest warden subsequently visited the nursery to help with technical problems. The Michigan Forestry Association occupied much of the discussion at the meeting, and the members of the Public Domain Commission urged the Forestry Association to continue its efforts and to cooperate with the commission in educating the public about the importance of forests.[19]

Among the most important areas identified in the new policy was fire protection, and the state's foresters set to work building fire lines. The lines were cleared of brush and stumps and were maintained with a disk pulled by a team of horses. Lines first were put in along section lines; each square-mile section was then divided; and finally each quarter section was divided again, resulting in a firebreak every quarter of a mile.

A headquarters was built at each state forest, with a residence for the custodian and his family and barns for the horses. Some compounds also included bunkhouses for workers, with the custodians (or their wives) expected to feed the laborers. Foresters had to cut and haul firewood for use at the headquarters. At first, obtaining supplies for building, cooking, or other purposes required the foresters to travel twenty or more miles with a team of horses, an endeavor that took the teams away from building fire lines, skidding firewood, plowing furrows for planting, and other work. Consequently, Schaaf argued in March 1917, the commission should purchase a Ford car for each of the state forests. The commissioners agreed, authorizing him to purchase four cars—one for each of the biggest forests—at $345 each, plus a truck body conversion attachment for the Higgins Lake vehicle at a cost of an additional $350.[20]

At the close of the 1915 fiscal year, the state forests totaled 235,000 acres in fifty-three tracts in fifty-three counties, with an additional 300,000 acres

∞ THE AGE OF THE AUTOMOBILE

On March 3, 1918, State Forester Marcus Schaaf wrote to Edward Zettle, superintendent of the Alpena State Forest, regarding the use of the new car that the state was providing for Zettle's use.

> As soon as the condition of the roads will permit, a car for official use will be delivered to your Forest by Mr. J. H. Dye, of Roscommon. I will inform you of the day on which he starts so that you can arrange to be at Headquarters when he arrives and learn to drive, if you do not already know how to handle a car.
>
> As a general rule it is expected that the Custodian, and he only, will drive the car and that he himself will keep it in repair and good running order. Unless something serious occurs, the car can be kept in good shape by a few minutes careful inspection at the end of each day to see that all nuts are tight, all parts running smoothly, etc. In other words it is not necessary to take it to a garage each time a spark plug becomes dirty, or some other little trouble occurs, and pay 60 or 75¢ per hour for work that any handy man can do just as well, and oft times better. Learn your car by driving it, and in case of trouble refer to the Manual. Do not attempt to speed, for Fords are not built for that purpose (and but very few men are). Twenty to twenty-three miles per hour on the best roads you have is fast enough. These among other things will help to keep the car in good order and add to its life.
>
> Strict account must be kept daily of the gas and oil used and the mileage run. A special form for this purpose will be furnished later. You are familiar enough with your territory to know the distances, so that a speedometer is not necessary.
>
> And please bear in mind that the car is not furnished for pleasure but for State business.

Source: Ralph R. Widner, ed., *Forests and Forestry in the American States: A Reference Anthology* (Missoula, Mont.: [National Association of State Foresters], 1968), 192–93.

---

of state lands in other classifications, which the members of the Public Domain Commission believed should be incorporated into the state forests. The commission estimated that its reforestation goals could be accomplished by planting 750 acres per year on each forest over the next sixty years. However, that rate was much higher than the current 750 acres total per year for all areas combined. The commissioners considered opening a second nursery to provide more trees for planting, but budget limitations

Stump field being reforested with pine seedlings by planting crews made up of local laborers, 1920. Courtesy of the Michigan Department of Natural Resources.

prevented them from doing so. Schaaf predicted that the state forest system would begin showing a profit by the time the planting was complete— around 1977.[21]

THE HIGGINS LAKE NURSERY, FOUNDED UNDER THE AUSPICES OF FILIBERT Roth and the Forestry Commission in 1903, continued to produce seedlings for reforestation in the state forests. In 1910, 6 acres were under cultivation, resulting in 124 acres of reforestation.[22] However, because trees in a nursery are close together and are well watered, diseases can spread easily, and Higgins Lake first faced this problem during the summer of 1914, when Schaaf reported finding what he referred to as *Peridermium cerebrum* in ponderosa and lodgepole pines, two species from the western United States being grown in the nursery. Schaaf and his personnel pulled all seedlings of those species from the nursery and burned them as well as those that had already been planted elsewhere. Schaaf subsequently called in Professors C. H. Kauffman and E. B. Maine of the University of Michigan, who identified the disease as sweet fern rust and recommended removal of sweet fern from the vicinity of the nursery.[23] The following year, Scotch pine at Beal's 1884

Transplanting seedlings at the Higgins Lake State Forest Nursery, Crawford County, 1913.

Grayling plantation were found to have the disease, which subsequently decimated those trees.[24]

Much of the work at the nursery was hand labor. Workers formed beds by placing sideboards along the edges with metal clips to hold them in place. Newly seeded beds were covered with screens to provide protection from sun and birds. All weeding was done manually. To reduce the time spent on construction of screens, Schaaf requested permission to purchase more durable cypress lumber, use of which might double the life expectancy of the screens. The commission responded that it would prefer to buy Michigan lumber.[25]

The sale of surplus nursery stock gradually became a substantial business. In 1917, Schaaf decided to require a minimum purchase of five hundred of any species to eliminate small purchases for ornamental purposes, which were labor-intensive: during wartime, obtaining workers was difficult.[26] Several foresters worked alone: Frank Van Sickle, custodian on the Fife Lake State Forest, planted eighteen acres by himself in the fall of 1918. Schaaf requested that the commission apply for draft deferments for forest custodians and the nursery superintendent, but the commissioners refused, saying that they would prefer to support the war effort.[27]

In addition to labor troubles, the nursery faced an invasion of white grubs (june bug larvae), which fed on seedlings' roots and caused considerable damage. To control the beetles, workers hung lanterns to attract flying adults, who would then fall into a pan of water suspended below the light. A second approach was to prick the nursery beds with a brush made from upholsterer's needles embedded in a board to prevent the larvae from maturing.[28]

The dearth of manpower evidently affected the private sector as well, and in July 1917, Wyman appeared before the commission to request that the state take over the fire protection services being performed by his Northern Forest Protective Association. He also recommended that a deputy be assigned to the Upper Peninsula with authority to place fire wardens in appropriate places and expressed an interest in being that deputy. The state could not name an additional deputy, but Wyman was named a "special assistant" with a salary of two thousand dollars per year, more than twice what the forest custodians earned. The following fall, the Michigan Hardwood Manufacturers' Association similarly relinquished its fire protection duties, although no "special assistant" was appointed in this case.[29]

Also in 1917, the state added to the reserves a two-hundred-acre parcel of virgin red and white pine timber known as Interlochen State Park.[30] The commission appointed a custodian who served only during fire weather and whose primary responsibility was to patrol the railroad tracks every time a train went through.[31] Duties added later included salvage of dead and down timber and release of young pines from overhead competition, with 114,000 board feet salvaged in January 1920.[32] In May, 1920, the land was transferred to the jurisdiction of the State Parks Commission, marking the beginning of the modern era of state parks in Michigan.[33] Many other state forest sites subsequently have been transferred to the state park system including North Higgins Lake, Clear Lake and Fisherman's Island State Parks.

The Public Domain Commission had accomplished much in its eleven years of management, but much still remained to be done. In 1920, several tracts—among them Kalkaska, Island Lake, Black Lake, Grayling, and Au Sable—still awaited opening for management.[34] During this period the state served as a good caretaker of the lands under its control, protecting them from fire, doing basic inventory, and initiating reforestation efforts. Forestry was also starting to blossom as a profession, with substantial applied research taking place at both the state and national levels.

5

State Government Reorganization

1921 – 1930

IN JULY 1919, THE PUBLIC DOMAIN COMMISSION ENGAGED PROFESSOR
Filibert Roth to make an inspection and report on conditions in northern
Michigan, more than fifteen years after creation of the first state forest reserves. He found promise, but the problem of forest fires still had not been
adequately addressed. The text of Roth's report was published in *Michigan
Sportsman* magazine. In a foreword to the published report, the secretary of
the Public Domain Commission, George L. Lusk, asked readers to give "serious consideration" to the matters of reforestation and wildlife conservation
but urged special attention to the "alarming and destructive" forest fires
that continued to plague the state. According to Lusk, "As far as state lands
are concerned, the policy of patrol and prompt action reduced the losses to
a minimum. Greater responsibility must be encouraged by the people as a
whole and more comprehensive preventive measures adopted."[1]

Roth opened the article by describing the beautiful scenery along his travels. Then, he wrote, his party headed "off for Newberry, a bright afternoon made smoky by fires. Never out of sight of smoke, most of the time in plain view of fresh, still burning fires. What a pity!" Roth provided readers with an estimate of the financial damage done by the fires, most of which occurred among second-growth timber. Replacing the trees would require either a planting cost of $7 per acre "plus waiting several years to get it to the size at which the stand was" or "waiting till nature replaces it, which will mean many years, many seasons' rent of the land, and in most cases will not be complete but only partial success and of much less value than the planting." Even if the cost were only $10 per acre, "the sum is big enough; it would and it *will* take several hundred thousand dollars to make good what we saw destroyed, and we saw only a small fraction of the total."[2]

Roth wanted to counter the argument, printed in numerous newspapers, that "the fires in the Soo district had been a great benefit and that all this fire talk was exaggeration." He accused some popularizers of that view of seeking "to hide their utter incompetence and that of the State and its agencies to cope with a truly serious situation, costing millions and hindering the development of Northern Michigan more than all other obstacles put together." In 1917–18, according to Roth, the fire warden's report showed that 521,000 acres of land had been burned, causing "damage (presumably to merchantable timber, logs, ties, poles, camps and farms only) of $243,000, and there was spent in fighting them the extravagant sum of $27,000. How much was done to organize and prepare for fires, to prevent fires, which is the only rational way to meet this evil, is not stated; nor is it given by what means the area was ascertained and the damage appraised. This sounds critical enough but it is not so meant at all, what is pertinent here is merely this: Michigan has lost several hundred millions of dollars and is losing millions again this year, besides being retarded in her development." In addition, Roth pointed out, the fires increased the problems caused by insects: "Every great fire season kills millions of birds and other helpful friends of the forests and gives the pests a new chance to spread."[3]

However, Roth argued, the fires could "be prevented any time that the people in their government really make up their minds to do so." As a "mark of forestry progress," Roth cited the state forest's "long, straight, clean, freshly disked [fire] lines, about 12 feet wide, perfectly competent to stop any ordinary ground fire in quiet weather; the "never-asleep" watchman of our cut-overs, the only way of preventing fires and the very best means of fighting fires if any do get away." He also suggested that "a little of the French idea might help,—there a tramp or person of unsavory reputation cannot go into any woods in dry times, and at no time is the public allowed off the roads leading through the woods; in addition, the negligent official who refuses to do his duty is not merely dismissed, but is properly punished."[4]

Roth closed the article with a plea to readers:

> We do not ask you to join anything or chip in. But do, please, look into this matter of forestry, think it over, and if you do agree with us, do not hesitate to say so; say it to your neighbor, say it to your representative and senator; let these men know that you favor it, and favor and approve the hearty support of these men in the legislature. Please keep in mind that only a third of the land in Michigan is improved today, that we have 12 million acres of cut-overs producing nothing when they should be growing at least 25 million dollars worth of wood per year,—that today Michigan imports more than half the timber her industries use, that at present rate of clearing it will be 500 years before we are cleared, and that this very year we are burning up millions of dollars in property and injure our good State for many years to come.
>
> Stand by forestry, it costs you nothing and will make a better, more prosperous State, more game and fish and more pleasant woods to roam.[5]

George "Jud" Madsen, a fire officer with the Michigan Department of Conservation, had similar memories of the fires during his boyhood in Newberry in the early twentieth century: "On summer evenings, there was a glow in the sky no matter which direction you looked. The woods was on fire, and nobody did anything about it."[6] Conditions on the state forests were improving through the efforts of the Public Domain Commission, but the area affected was relatively small and little progress had been made in bringing management and fire protection to all of the state's forests and forest reserves. A reorganization of state government was in the wind, once again offering new leadership for the state forests.

A series of articles in the *Detroit News* in May 1920 described the state's forest situation and some of what still needed to be done. While conditions on the state forests had improved, what had been accomplished represented an almost insignificant proportion of the state's problem. Professor P. S. Lovejoy of the University of Michigan wrote the first article in the *Detroit News* series. He opened with the observation that "a third of Michigan virtually is bankrupt, unable to pay its way with schools and roads, getting poorer instead of richer from year to year, producing less and less of value." He contrasted the Michigan experience to that of neighboring Ohio, which had also been a heavily forested state but remained prosperous even after most of the timber had been cut. Lovejoy detailed the amount of Michigan owned by large landholders who were evasive about why they held such cutover lands while making no effort at protection or management, then cited the "sucker industry" that sold such lands to immigrants for farmland. He noted that the secretary of the Public Domain Commission was also the immigration commissioner. These facts had not changed since the report of the Commission of Inquiry some eleven years earlier. Thus, forestry advocates were less than pleased with the status of Michigan's forest resources at the dawn of the 1920s.[7]

Uncontrolled fire remained the biggest obstacle to progress in forestry. An estimated half million acres burned every year, and fires repeatedly burned the same areas until the soil fertility was gone and nothing remained to carry a fire. A dual system of fire protection had developed—one for the state forests, under the administration of the state forester, and one for the other millions of acres of Michigan's forests, under the administration of the state fish, game, and forest fire warden, whose interest in game management overrode any interest in fire protection, according to *Detroit News* reporter Fred Janette, who wrote ten articles printed in May–June 1920. He cited false economy in the Fish, Game, and Fire Department—spending less than $100,000 per year in fire control costs while losing more than $750,000 annually in soil and timber.[8]

Michigan's fire laws were less effective than those in other states, particularly in the areas of fire prevention and slash disposal. And while discussion continued, so did the fires—at a rate equivalent to an entire county every year. Michigan conservationist and author James Oliver Curwood described Michigan as the "worst burned state in the country" in a September 1921 article in *American Forestry*. That article went on to say that Michigan was losing $50 million per year from fire and lack of effort to control it.[9]

According to forest historian Norman J. Schmaltz, Parrish Storrs Lovejoy (1884–1942) was "perhaps the single most persuasive voice in the cause of state forestry for Michigan in the pre–World War II period."

Born in 1884, Lovejoy came from a family of activists. His grandfather was an abolitionist, and his great uncle, Elijah Parrish Lovejoy, an Alton, Illinois, journalist, is known as "a martyr on the Altar of American Liberty." Elijah Lovejoy was killed by a mob who wanted Lovejoy to stop writing antislavery articles.

Lovejoy studied forestry under Filibert Roth at the University of Michigan and after graduating went west to work for Gifford Pinchot's Forest Service in Wyoming and Washington, returning to teach at the university in 1912. Dissatisfied with academic life, Lovejoy quit in 1920 and spent three years as a freelance writer, sounding the clarion call for conservation. A frequent contributor to the *Country Gentleman*, a weekly farm magazine, he wrote several articles about regulating the unscrupulous real estate activity on forest lands, the need for reforestation of cutover lands and land use planning.

In 1923 he joined the Michigan Department of Conservation, working on the Land Economic Survey as its first director. Lovejoy envisioned a statewide resource inventory that would record the soil, land cover, wildlife, and recreation situation in northern Michigan. Involved in all aspects of land use, he continued to write popular articles for a variety of magazines. One of his best known is "The Michigan Timberland Tax Law," which he wrote in 1925 for *Southern Lumberman*. He later served as chief of the Game Division and as a member of the blue-ribbon Advisory Forest Committee that was created in 1931 to make recommendations regarding Michigan's forest conservation agenda.

After suffering a serious stoke in 1931 he returned to work and continued to advise the department on land use issues. He died in 1942. His ashes were scattered in the Pigeon River Country State Forest where a simple monument is inscribed "P. S. Lovejoy, 1884–1942."

Despite the valiant efforts of a handful of foresters and forestry advocates, the state's forestry program continued to receive only a fraction of the political support and funding it needed to thrive.

In addition to ongoing concerns such as fire, new items continually joined the list of problems facing Michigan's forests. Exotic pests such as the Japanese beetle, white pine blister rust, and chestnut blight had appeared on the scene and were drawing nationwide attention. Many forestry experts viewed white pine blister rust as the last nail in the coffin of the pine, believing that white pine could not be produced again in Michigan in commercial quantities.

EARLY IN 1921, GOVERNOR ALEX GROESBECK SUBMITTED TO THE LEGISLA-ture a plan for reorganizing the state government. He proposed the creation of a new department to assume the functions of the Public Domain Commission, none of whose members, he pointed out, "were elected because of any technical knowledge they possessed concerning conservation problems." "If you see fit," he told the legislature, "to supplant the present system with one organized on up to date lines, it is suggested that, among other things, there should be at least three divisions of the same, namely, forests and parks, fish and game, waters and waterways, so that its membership may be selected with reference to their qualifications for each kind of service."[10]

The legislature responded swiftly, creating the Department of Conservation early in 1921. The department's new Forestry and Silviculture Division took charge of the forestry program, and Marcus Schaaf remained in the position of state forester. Groesbeck appointed John Baird as the department's first director and named Roth as one of the first members of the Conservation Commission. The seven member Commission was the policy making body of the Department. Fred Z. Pantlind of Grand Rapids, an active member of the Michigan Forestry Association, also received an appointment to the commission, and Groesbeck named W. H. Wallace of Saginaw to chair the commission.

In August 1921, the Conservation Commission met at the custodian's residence at Fife Lake and toured the Fife Lake, Houghton Lake, and Higgins Lake State Forests. While there, Schaaf called attention to the lack of school opportunities for the custodians' families, particularly at the Pigeon River Forest. Baird promised to take up the matter with the state superintendent of instruction.[11]

The Conservation Department began almost immediately after its formation to amass a system of state parks and game refuges. P. J. Hoffmaster, chief of the State Parks Division, zealously led the effort. Six hundred acres of state forest in Emmet County were exchanged for 1.5 miles of Lake Michigan shoreline that became the Lake Michigan Game Refuge. Although the state lost money based on timber and land values, the desirability of the Lake Michigan shore offset any financial disadvantage. The state's interest seemed to lie in parks and refuges rather than with the more mundane state forests.

The Michigan Forestry Association, long a supporter of forestry in general and the state forests in particular, soon grew impatient with the new agency. In its 1925 report to its members, the association criticized the state fire warden's latest report, accusing him of concealing the true cost of the damage caused by forest fires. The association took some solace in the governor's approval of an experiment in "complete fire protection"—hiring year-round fire wardens and equipping them with trucks stocked with fire-fighting equipment.[12] Association Secretary John C. DeCamp reported in the group's August 1925 newsletter,

> The State is waking up. Forestry is becoming recognized as a practicable use for poor soils. The various interests affected by timber depletion are learning to cooperate with each other and with the Department of Conservation. The Dept., for its part, is evidently at last awake to the need for building up within its organization a corps of competent forestry experts.
>
> The Pearson Act was slower than we expected in getting started. The fire season was a shock—we planted 6,000 acres and burned 700,000. We need most of all and first of all, adequate fire protection. We need wise leadership, free from political or selfish interests.
>
> Possibly also we need protection from friends too busy bewailing approaching timber famine to feel the surge of awakening consciousness in reforestation. Michigan may have given of her timber. She may have been devastated by fires. Her cut-over lands may be bankrupt. But she has left in her lakes and her streams an asset greater than the timber ever was. Given back her forests, what State so rich in recreational facilities?
>
> Timber famine is a far-off problem; human ingenuity may yet solve it. The immediate problem is to protect our recreational values through growing trees on barren lands. This problem calls for quick action and promises quick returns. It is a problem of the people themselves. A great State is waking up to its possibilities.[13]

As part of an effort to reestablish wildlife in northern Michigan, the department devised a plan to introduce reindeer into the Upper Peninsula. In 1922, a three-thousand-acre enclosure was constructed in the Lake Superior State Forest, near the headquarters on Muskallonge Lake, to serve as a home for the reindeer, recently imported from Norway. In February 1923, Pantlind moved that the Lake Superior State Forest be abandoned as a forest and made into a state game reserve "for the reason that conditions that have existed in the past have made this necessary for the preservation and the economical administration of this reserve." This move was evidently a mere formality, since the transfer of the reindeer had already taken place.[14]

David R. Jones of the Conservation Department described the transfer of the reindeer in an article in the February 15, 1923, issue of *The Michigan Sportsman*. He explained that the reindeer, sixty-one in all, were purchased from Norway in 1922 for $125 each. They had been held at the Mason Game Farm in southern Michigan for a while, and then were moved to the Hanson Game Reserve near Grayling, but were not sustaining themselves well at that location. It was therefore deemed important to transfer them to the enclosure that had been constructed for them near Newberry as soon as possible. The animals were moved by rail from Grayling to Newberry; then to Underwood's Camp, about twelve miles out of town on the Charcoal Iron Company Road. Having arrived at Newberry around noon and Underwood's Camp sometime later, there was no time to waste in moving the herd on toward headquarters, as they were all tired and hungry. Things began to deteriorate as the hapless herd made its way north toward its destination. Said Jones: "As it was getting dark it was impossible to keep the entire herd under control and they scattered badly during the night, and as it snowed some, it took several hours to round them up the following day. Some of them were picked up at least three miles from Underwood's Camp and near the railroad leading to Newberry." Still tired and hungry, the bedraggled immigrants reached their new home on the second day and seemed to adjust rather well. There was reportedly an abundance of reindeer moss at the new location.

The rest of the story was told in the Department's Biennial Report for 1927 and 28: "It is not clear from the official reports just what subsequently happened but the reindeer did not thrive. Some fawns were born but most of them died young and the adult animals began to die from a trouble described as having symptoms similar to those of spinal meningitis: partial paralysis and the like. It was thought that some deficiency of diet might be involved, but no complete diagnosis appears to have been made, and such treatments as were tried did not succeed in saving the herd." A federal bulletin was quoted as saying the stock was inferior to Siberian reindeer that had been successfully introduced in Alaska.

It was rumored after this that people had seen bands of reindeer in the pinelands north of Newberry during the winters, but none of these reports was confirmed. The reindeer experiment was declared a failure in 1927.[15] At the same time, the Lake Superior Game Reserve was again made a state forest.

In 1925, Schaaf identified a need for authority to sell mature timber from the state lands: "The sale and utilization of mature timber is not only a strong argument for greater efforts in reforestration [sic] by the State, but it is, in the final analysis, the only argument which justifies the existence of the State Forests." The Conservation Commission agreed and in February 1925 recommended preparation and introduction of a bill giving the commission authorization to sell mature timber from the state forests.[16] The legislature granted the requested authority, and the department's biennial report for 1927–28 announced, "Marketing of mature green timber from the State Forests was undertaken for the first time in 1928 at the Fife Lake place. While, of course, no large tracts of merchantable timber occur on the State lands, there are individual clumps and remnants that may as well be utilized. Scattered as it is, this material cannot be logged at any great profit, but it will bring in some revenue and its removal leaves the Forest in better condition. Operations were confined to jack pine pulpwood, of which some 450 cords were taken off, bringing an average of $6.60 on cars."[17] This watershed event testified to the value of protecting and managing the cutover, abandoned wastelands and constituted a major policy change.

Improvements were made on the forests, including four-room cottages built on the Higgins Lake, Houghton Lake, Ogemaw, Alpena, and Presque Isle Forests to house hired men and their families, and modern water systems installed on the Presque Isle and Pigeon River. Four million trees were planted in 1921, with 2 million more planted in 1922.[18]

The Higgins Lake Nursery continued its crucial role in providing stock for planting. A one-hundred-thousand-gallon holding tank was installed on the hill north of the nursery for irrigation. Disease problems were alleviated through improved sanitation—no mulching, no shade, and fall sowing. Total reforestation on the state forests stood at just over twelve thousand acres in 1922, and two years later the Conservation Department decided to double the nursery's capacity. U.S. Forest Service Chief William Greeley visited in 1926 and pronounced it "the best-managed, largest in output and altogether the finest coniferous forest nursery in America."[19]

As welcome as the attention must have been, the nursery expansion plan caused Schaaf concern. In response to the order to double the capacity, Schaaf pointed out that Fife Lake and Ogemaw would be planted up in two years, and at least one other forest was close behind. To have a place to plant the increased numbers of seedlings, more state land would need to be placed under management.[20]

IN 1926, THE DEDICATED FOREST RESERVES INCLUDED 361,000 ACRES, BUT only 120,000 acres had been opened up and placed under management. Schaaf left no doubt as to where he stood on the matter. "Three hundred sixty-one thousand acres of Forest Reserve land, and less than half of this actually under management, is not a very large percentage of the State-owned acreage." He estimated that 15 million acres under various owners needed reclamation and asserted that the state should be taking the lead in reestablishing forests. Schaaf argued, "The ultimate goal should be not less than five or six million acres. Michigan must think of State Forests in terms of millions of acres instead of thousands!"[21] The state forests' acreage growth stagnated, but the parks and game reserves were gaining momentum, with approximately 65,000 acres in nine refuges in 1926.[22]

Nevertheless, substantial progress was being made on the state forests that had been dedicated. The department launched a system of forest campgrounds with the 1929 creation of the Spring Lake Campground on the Fife Lake State Forest. The following year, campgrounds were established on Muskallonge Lake, Higgins Lake, Black Lake, and the south branch of the Thunder Bay River. "The intention [was] to maintain these grounds in as natural a condition as possible by avoiding too much artificiality and equipping them with the barest of necessities only, as stoves, tables, toilets, wells and boats."[23] Thus, although state forest acreage was not expanding, the management of dedicated areas was developing into a policy of multiple uses. Still, a way was needed to build the forestry program by putting more acres under management.

A Grand Rapids man, Frederick Wheeler, owned a farm near Williamsburg, in Grand Traverse County, where he spent a good deal of time. Near the farm was an untold amount of cutover land that had once produced good quality timber but that had subsequently burned repeatedly. The landscape was desolate, but Wheeler saw its potential if someone could be persuaded to care enough about it to protect it from fire and perhaps plant a few trees.

Around 1911, Wheeler began acquiring this land. Whether he intended from the outset to donate it to the state is unclear, but in 1930 he gave to the state several thousand acres in Grand Traverse and Kalkaska Counties. Wheeler subsequently attempted to persuade other landowners to donate holdings to the state "without any cash return so this is not a money-making proposition for us." The donated land would become known as "memorial forests" and was to be used for the public good in perpetuity. One tract of more than three thousand acres was designated the Abraham Lincoln Memorial Forest, while other blocks were dedicated in memory of various Wheeler ancestors.

The *Grand Rapids Herald* noted Wheeler's gift of land in an April 1930 editorial: "It is rather refreshing to run into a case where the owner of very desirable lands lying in a state forest reserve area believed it his duty to help the state in rounding out its holdings and deliberately deeded his lands to the state without any financial remuneration. The only string tied to the gift was, that the state must reforest the land with pine trees, which really is the only reason the state wanted them." The *Detroit News* also recognized Wheeler's generosity and subsequently sponsored its own reforestation program. Other additions to the system soon began to pour in, but not in the manner that Wheeler had anticipated.

6

The Great Depression

1931–1940

As the Department of Conservation neared the end of its first decade, observers took stock of its progress. Some former critics now gave credit to the new organization and its accomplishments. The creation of a citizen commission to oversee the department, they felt, insulated the agency from problems responsible for past abuses. In its September 6, 1930, newsletter, the Michigan Forestry Association commented, "Much of our advance in reforestation has been made possible by taking the Conservation Department out of politics. It is now being agitated that we return to the old system of governor-controlled appointments. Such a step backward is unthinkable."[1]

The Conservation Department held together through the rough economic times that dominated the 1930s, although employees' salaries were reduced by the Conservation Commission in January 1932 and again by the legislature six months later.[2] In its 1932 annual report, the department observed that the three classes of public land under its jurisdiction—game refuges, state parks, and state forests—were "tending toward common objectives." The report noted that "a well handled game refuge would in time produce considerable merchantable timber; a well handled state forest would normally produce much game, and both might include good fishing water."[3] The recreational use of state project lands was becoming the dominant consideration.

In pursuit of this multiplicity of uses, in 1931 the department established the Pigeon River State Forest as a first effort to "devise and apply a plan for the parallel and harmonious development and utilization of all the resources upon a large and varied tract." The tract was started with seven thousand acres of tax-reverted poor pineland, to which were added about forty-five thousand acres of purchased game land on which elk, transported from the western United States, had been released in 1918. And rounding out the picture were some twenty miles of the Pigeon River included in the tract. The plan for management said in part, "There shall be *parallel* and *harmonious* development and utilization of *all* the various resources—economic, aesthetic recreational, [which] would seem to mark a new and material advance in conservation concept and practice."[4]

Developments on the public lands contrasted with a general lack of progress in most of rural Michigan. Contrary to popular expectations, the plow had not followed the axe, at least not in any meaningful way, in much of the northern part of the state. Two million acres had reverted to state ownership for nonpayment of taxes during the 1920s, and the end was not in sight in 1932.[5] Several state-owned tracts were established as game refuges to provide some opportunity for wildlife populations to recover from the market hunting and loss of habitat that had taken place over the previous three or four decades. More than four hundred thousand acres were closed to hunting in 1932, including five thousand acres at Cusino in the Upper Peninsula, a whole township on the Pigeon River tract, and two townships in Roscommon County.[6]

CONCERN FOR THE OVERALL FOREST MANAGEMENT PROGRAM, THE INcreased tax-reverted lands and the potential forest industry became evident on June 12, 1931, when the Michigan Conservation Commission adopted the following resolution:

WHEREAS, The State of Michigan has for nearly thirty years been engaged in a program of reforesting cut-over and idle lands, with approximately 100,000 acres planted to date, and surrounded by miles of firelines; and

WHEREAS, the State ownership of cut-over lands has been increasing rapidly and promises to increase still faster during the next decade; and

WHEREAS, the forms in which wood is utilized have been changing and the recreational values of forests and forest lands and their relationship to fish, game, and other wild life have recently assumed large economic importance; and

WHEREAS, a marked reduction in the funds available for State forest activities during the next biennium has been made by the legislature;

THEREFORE, BE IT RESOLVED, That the time is auspicious for checking over our forests and forest land affairs; and that the Chairman be requested to appoint a committee of outstanding competence to inquire into and report, with recommendations, on what has been accomplished to date, and as to modifications of plans and procedure which may be in order for the future.

Commission Chairman William H. Loutit appointed the members of the Forest Advisory Committee. It was chaired by E. W. Tinker, regional forester, (Region 9) United States Forest Service, Milwaukee, Wisconsin. Members included Paul A. Herbert, chair, Department of Forestry, Michigan Agricultural College, East Lansing; Samuel Trask Dana, professor of forestry and dean of the School of Forestry and Conservation, University of Michigan, Ann Arbor; and Raphael Zon, director, Lakes States Forest Experiment Station, St. Paul, Minnesota. Several staff members from the agency worked with the committee for over a year including Commissioner Harold Titus, State Forester Marcus Schaaf, and P. S. Lovejoy.

Tinker submitted the final report to Department Director George Hogarth on January 10, 1933. It contained twenty-one summary points. Some of the more important recommendations were that the care and improvement of existing stands of timber through release cuttings in plantations and natural stands of white and red pine was an essential part of forest management; reforestation was essential for the reclamation of large areas of state land and should be continued to the extent permitted by the capacity of the Higgins Lake Nursery; and additional research is greatly needed in the areas of fire control, timber production, game management, and recreation.

In the conclusion to the advisory committee's report to the commission they stated "So far as State lands are concerned, our chief recommendations are that the Department of Conservation concentrate its efforts on the intensive development of lands organized into definite State Conservation areas; that these be handled under comprehensive management plans providing for the coordinated use of all resources; and that the field personnel be built up to the point where it can assume primary responsibility for the preparation and execution of these plans. Such a program, adequately financed and efficiently administered. . . . will constitute a most effective contribution to the solution of northern Michigan's land problem."

Even though the state forests were beginning to demonstrate their potential to serve the public through timber production and recreation opportunities, forestry still had its detractors. Critics charged that the state was impeding progress by taking land off the tax rolls and thus reducing local government revenue. These criticisms and the double salary reductions of 1932 cast a pall over the future of the state forests. Even nursery production had to be scaled down "due to the State's rigid program of economy inaugurated in 1931."[7]

Then came a breath of fresh air. In 1933, at the behest of President Franklin D. Roosevelt, Congress authorized emergency conservation work "for employing citizens of the United States who are unemployed, in the construction, maintenance, and carrying on of works of a public nature in connection with the forestation of land . . . the prevention of forest fires, floods, and soil erosion, plant pest and disease control, the construction, maintenance or repair of paths, trails, and fire lanes [for the] purpose of relieving the acute condition of widespread distress and unemployment . . . and to provide for the restoration of the country's depleted natural resources and the advancement of an orderly program of useful public works." The Civilian Conservation Corps (CCC) was born in the spring of 1933.[8] The CCC gave the state forests a new lease on life.

Michigan's first state forest CCC camp opened May 22, 1933, at Higgins Lake and was followed a few days later by a camp at Wolverine in Cheboygan County. Through mid-July, camps were created at various other sites in Michigan, with the last forestry camp opening on July 18 in the Pigeon River State Forest. Camps existed on all state forests except Alpena. A total of forty-two state forestry camps existed during the program's first year—twelve on the state forests, three on the state game refuges, and twenty-seven on unadministered state and private forests. In its first year, the CCC built and/or improved 500 miles of roads in Michigan, built 120 miles of fire lines, accomplished many stream improvement projects, built fire towers, and modernized and expanded buildings and equipment. CCC crews also constructed new campgrounds at Twin Lakes in the Black Lake State Forest, Big Tomahawk Lake in the Presque Isle State Forest, Ambrose Lake in the Ogemaw State Forest, Muskallonge Lake in the Lake Superior State Forest, and on the Muskegon River on the Houghton Lake State Forest.[9]

More than 7,500 men worked in the forty-two camps, plus 425 supervisory and training personnel. The Department of War took care of logistics—camp setup, subsistence, clothing, and medical care—and the Forest Service selected locations and coordinated projects, supervision, supplies, and materials.[10] It was a massive project, but then, so was the scale of the problem to which it was addressed.

The CCC is perhaps most famous for its tree planting, but its workers planted no trees at all in Michigan in the spring of 1933. As a consequence of previous cutbacks in nursery operations, there were no trees to plant. By the end of June 1934, however, the CCC had planted more than 20,000 acres, bringing the state forest total to more than 140,000 acres. The preferred method of site preparation for planting was furrowing with a tractor and plow, but all the heavy equipment was engaged in road projects, so sod was removed by hand from the entire 20,000 acres planted in 1933–34. Lineal survey was pushed as rapidly as possible to identify boundaries of state-owned lands and preserve the work done by government surveyors nearly a hundred years earlier. CCC surveyors completed 1,146 miles of "random lines" (so named because they rarely hit their exact intended location) and corrected another 225 miles of lines.[11]

After two years, the CCC crews had built more than 2,500 miles of roads and 265 bridges spanning between twelve and two hundred feet. They had performed white pine blister rust control on more than 184,000 acres by hand pulling gooseberry plants. They had accomplished fish habitat improvement on 2,500 acres of lakes and 275 miles of trout streams. They had surveyed groundwater conditions on nearly 3 million acres.[12]

Activities more directly related to timber management included a timber reconnaissance program started in June 1934 that involved one forester and a CCC crew for each forest in the Lower Peninsula. In addition, at about the same time, timber stand improvement (the thinning of hardwood stands and the releasing of pines from overhead competition) was undertaken. At the time, this work was considered experimental, because no data yet showed that it would enhance the growth of pines, but it seemed logical and provided work that could be done during the winter, when most other projects had to be suspended, so officials decided to go ahead. Test plots were established to monitor the success of the practice. A total of twelve hundred acres underwent timber stand improvement during the first biennium.[13]

Fire control and prevention remained a major concern on all of Michigan's forestlands. During its first two years, the CCC performed fire hazard reduction work on nearly eighteen thousand acres, mostly felling snags and piling brush to prevent fire from carrying across the ground. CCC crews also added to the "eyes of the forest" by constructing twelve steel fire towers, spent sixty-one thousand man-days fighting more than six hundred fires, and constructed concrete block warehouses for fire equipment at Marquette and Roscommon.[14] As part of the fire control effort, forests were mapped and fire officers and other personnel received radios. Bulldozers were employed to build fire lines. Fire officers and conservation officers developed master plans for fire protection, assessing response time, fire hazards, and available personnel and equipment. Eighteen thousand acres burned in 1935, "by far the lowest acreage lost since records have been kept." The following year, however, represented one of the worst fire hazards in history: fifty thousand acres burned, and so much smoke hung in the air that the fire towers were useless.[15]

BIG AS IT WAS, THE CCC'S REFORESTATION PROGRAM DID NOT ACCOMplish all the needed planting. In 1930, the *Detroit News* initiated sponsorship

One of many Detroit News *plantations established through donations from the public starting in 1930. The program ran for more than ten years, and more than fifteen thousand acres were planted. Courtesy of the Michigan Department of Natural Resources.*

of a planting program under which donors could contribute $100 to cover the cost of planting forty acres. The state would provide the trees, supervise the planting, and maintain the forest in good condition. The *News* would provide an "indestructible" steel sign identifying the donor or the person in whose honor the trees had been planted. The program ran until 1942, when labor shortages caused by World War II meant that workers could no longer be found. During the more than ten years for which the program ran, more than $40,000 (a figure all the more notable because the period included the height of the Great Depression) was collected and some fifteen thousand acres were planted. Because state officials often managed to keep the cost of planting the trees below the estimate of $2.50 per acre, the surplus was used to plant memorial forests honoring U.S. presidents and Michigan governors. In addition to Frederick Wheeler (see chapter 5), notable donors to the program included a man named Kepsel whose memorial forest covered 2,640 acres and the Michigan Branch of the Daughters of the American Revolution.[16]

The Michigan Daughters of the American Revolution had begun their support of reforestation with a donation to be used for a land purchase somewhere in the Mackinac State Forest in 1929 and continued to back tree planting as late as 1969, when, according to the *Roscommon Herald-News*, the "society provided $1,400 for the planting of some 46,000 trees on approximately 40 acres in Houghton Lake State Forest." In response to a 1957 DAR inquiry, Glenn Schaap of the Conservation Department's Forestry Division wrote, "According to our records the Michigan Branch of the Daughters of the American Revolution have donated money for the planting of 21 descriptions (40 acre parcels) on state forests. The species of trees planted consisted chiefly of red pine, only a few jack pine and white pine were planted. It is estimated that approximately 480 acres were planted with approximately 525,000 trees."[17]

These tree-planting efforts faced some substantial hurdles. Bad weather during several years in the 1930s led to the failure of many of the plantations. However, many of these failed plots were subsequently replanted, and most eventually grew to be quite impressive. By the early 1950s, even most failed sites were occupied by well-established forest growth of some kind, precluding further efforts to replant pines.

The signs marking the *Detroit News* plots also continually caused problems. Although the paper assumed responsibility for the markers, the forest superintendents had to keep track of their condition and report signs needing replacement. As a consequence of natural wear and tear as well as the fact that hunters seemed to find the signs irresistible targets, it proved impossible to maintain the signs, and in 1955 R. G. Auble, assistant state forester, ordered their removal, although some in remote locations were missed and continued to mark sites as late as the 1970s.[18]

At the turn of the twenty-first century, the *Detroit News* plantations are now reaching maturity, and numerous stands have been harvested and replanted. Some of the better-known areas planted by this program are near Rexton in Mackinac County, near Weber Lake in Cheboygan County, the Pigeon River County area, and northeast of St. Helen in Ogemaw County. The program would have to be considered a success.

WHILE THE RECONSTRUCTION WORK WAS UNDER WAY ON THE PUBLIC lands under the aegis of the U.S. Department of Agriculture's Forest Service, another branch of the department was working on Michigan's forest problem from a different perspective, under authority of the Bankhead-Jones Farm Tenant Act. The Resettlement Administration undertook four large projects in Michigan aimed at helping farmers relocate from submarginal farmland.[19] As the *Plainwell Enterprise* drily observed in 1935, "Michigan residents have been hesitant to admit that some of the land is not suited to farming." Under the resettlement project, owners of such unsuitable lands were offered fair market value for their holdings as well as sufficient credit to begin farming elsewhere. Bills in the state legislature then permitted rezoning of the land to prevent further attempts at agricultural use.[20]

In October 1935, the *Enterprise* reported on one of the largest farm-to-forest conversion projects, which involved thirty-five thousand acres in west-central Allegan County that the Resettlement Administration purchased for about $118,000. The administration's regional director, Reynolds I. Nowell, described the plight of the people who were trying to farm the land:

Living on infertile soil, in a virtual forest [frost] pocket which tremendously shortens the growing season, are 120 families. . . . They are mostly squatters, many of whom came here in their desperation to occupy abandoned buildings when the depression was forcing them into bread-lines elsewhere. Some others, who formerly worked at one trade or another in the cities, bought land there "sight unseen" because the prospect of getting back into the country sounded so attractive when the salesman talked to them about it.

They are too far from industrial centers to get jobs, and they can't earn enough through farming. Average annual family income in this region is $200–$300. Half of that comes from welfare agencies.

Standards of living are desperately low, although county nurses and county agricultural agents have done their best to help these people. One family with seven children is living in a shack with no floor.[21]

Over the next five years, the Resettlement Administration proceeded with the project, and in 1940 the federal government leased the Allegan County lands to the state of Michigan for ninety-five years. The Michigan Department of Conservation assumed management of the land, which became the Allegan State Forest.[22]

MICHIGAN'S ONGOING FIRE PROBLEM LED TO A SWELLING OF THE STATE'S deer population, which thrived in the dense, brushy habitats that arose in the wake of fire.[23] In the absence of adequate control, dense deer populations can strip their habitat of food, and by 1935, the Department of Conservation listed deer starvation as its biggest wildlife problem. Areas closed to hunting on the state game areas were reduced in size, but the problem continued to build. The Conservation Department noted in 1936 that wildlife managers "must broaden [their] thinking beyond just increasing populations, as some areas are at capacity."[24] Nevertheless, the situation continued to worsen, and in 1938 wildlife researchers at Cusino, in Alger County, began formal deer nutrition studies to gain insights on dealing with the problem.[25]

By 1936, the state had sixteen game areas totaling more than 811,000 acres. Six of the game areas—Crawford, Cusino, Escanaba River, Iosco, Lunden, and Ogemaw—had resident superintendents. Five (Alpena, Butterfield [in Roscommon and Missaukee Counties], Molasses River, Otsego, and Pigeon River) were administered in cooperation with the Forestry Division, and another five (Cedar River, Drummond Island, Gladwin, Luther-Baldwin, and Midland) fell under some other administrative arrangement.[26]

In the winters of 1934–35 and 1935–36, the state transferred forty-six moose from Isle Royale to the mainland at Keweenaw, Cusino, Escanaba River, and the Detroit Zoo. Sharptail grouse were also transplanted. The first sharptails had been noted in the western Upper Peninsula around 1920 and by 1938 had spread eastward to Marquette and Dickinson Counties. Fifty-one birds were caught and moved to Chippewa County, near Trout Lake, and twenty-one more were moved to the Pigeon River forest. Further stocking of sharptails took place at eight locations in 1940. Game management was truly experiencing phenomenal growth. In 1936, the department established a hardwood nursery, managed by the Forestry Division, on forty acres in Charlevoix County to produce trees and shrubs for wildlife habitat planting.[27]

Because of the dire economic conditions that prevailed in the early 1930s, a property tax moratorium was enacted between 1933 and 1937, and taxes owed from 1932 and earlier could be paid in ten annual installments. During this period, no lands reverted to the state. By 1940, however, tax reversions were again taking place, and the state owned more than 5 million

Gathering of forest superintendents at Pigeon River Fisheries Experiment Station, Otsego County, February 1940. From left: Marcus Schaaf, state forester; Grover Zettle, Ogemaw State Forest; James Finley, Hardwood State Forest; Ed Zettle, Higgins Lake Nursery; Bernard McTiver, Lake Superior State Forest; Merle Prichard, Presque Isle State Forest; Dave Green, Black Lake State Forest; Bill Horsell, Pigeon River State Forest; Anthony Sullivan, Houghton Lake State Forest; C. J. Morey, Alpena State Forest; Forrest Clark, Mackinac State Forest; Max Lange, Au Sable State Forest; George McIntire, assistant state forester; Frank Van Sickle, Fife Lake State Forest. Courtesy of the State Archives of Michigan; photo by Norman F. Smith.

acres, including more than 1 million acres classified as state forest and a similar amount classified as game areas. The Conservation Department predicted that if the 1939 tax reversion rate were to continue, 30 percent of the state's land would be under public ownership by 1965.[28]

Along with the growth in acres and the increased success of the fire control program came a significant increase in timber volume and value on the state forestland. The Forestry Division's 1939–40 biennial report noted "an almost imperceptible shift in emphasis from a program of reclamation and building to one of more complete utilization of what is now available." Moreover, the report continued, "nearly forty years ago when the State Forest system was started the one idea was the re-building of a depleted forest resource. Today the main objectives in the management of the State Forests are the production of timber, the providing of recreation, and, following as a result of these, the creation of economic stability."[29]

7

The War Years

1941–1946

Conservation Department Director P. J. Hoffmaster, in his preface to the department's biennial report for 1941–42, described the effects of the war effort on his department as "profound." "Many activities have been necessarily curtailed because of lack of trained men," he said, noting that valued employees were engaged in the war effort.[1]

Department budgets were strained as license sales sagged and park attendance dropped. What few able-bodied men were around were working six or seven days a week and had little time for hunting. Conservation officers' duties were expanded to cover the department's fire-fighting responsibility. Many were named rural fire committee chairmen and spent most of the summer of 1942 writing fire plans.

The Forestry Division suffered the same shortage of staff, while demand for forest products skyrocketed, resulting in a doubling of timber harvested from the state forests from 1941 to 1942.[2] The Department of

Conservation printed a poster that showed a forest road bracketed by trees of various sizes and species and urged, "KEEP 'EM GROWING! HELP WIN THE WAR." Nursery stock was disposed of, as there was no one to plant it. The Conservation Commission deferred until after the war additional funds offered for operation of the nursery.[3] No trees were planted in the spring of 1942, signaling the end of the Civilian Conservation Corps and the *Detroit News* planting programs, and a year later, the Conservation Commission passed a resolution discontinuing reforestation efforts on the state forests until the end of the war or "until such time as labor and funds are again available."[4]

Responding to the increased pressure to harvest timber on the state lands and to reports of the thousands of acres in need of reforestation, Hoffmaster noted, "We are now obligated to use extreme caution in the custody of our resources, that there might remain after the war something on which to rebuild."[5] Shorthanded or not, the Forestry Division had work to do, and the remaining staff pitched in to do it.

Adding further to the workload on the state forests during the war was the large increase in state forest acreage. In the department's 1941–42 report, State Forester Marcus Schaaf noted that the state forests continued to expand through tax reversion, purchase, and exchange. Nearly 500,000 acres were added through tax reversion in 1939 and 1940, and by June 1942, the state forests included a total of 1,851,320 acres—nearly 5 percent of the state's total land and 10 percent of its forested land.[6]

Early in 1943, department officials noted that lumber and pulpwood production both nationwide and in Michigan had dropped off significantly and realized that they would have to help those industries if the flow of critical wood products to the defense plants and armed forces was to be maintained.[7] The Michigan State Forestry Committee outlined an action program to address this problem, using money obtained through the Timber Production War Project.

The War Production Board had made funds available to the U.S. Forest Service to set up the Timber Production War Project to assist the forest products industry in all states east of the Great Plains. Under the direction of area forester Charles H. Burton, the former assistant director of the Civilian Conservation Corps in Michigan, the state was divided into thirty project areas, each headed by a project forester taken from the ranks of state forest superintendents, game area managers, national forest rangers, farm foresters, soil conservationists, and other foresters. This work represented an addition to their regular duties. Timber Production War Project foresters contacted local draft boards and U.S. Employment Service offices, located parts and equipment, investigated truck and tractor applications, secured supplemental gasoline, located markets or stumpage, and interpreted government orders and regulations. The project recorded "very favorable" results during its first year.[8]

THE FORESTRY DIVISION'S BUDGET CONTAINED NO MONEY FOR MAINTENANCE and repair of roads and bridges, and in the early 1940s they were in very poor condition. This situation gave rise to frequent public criticism of the division.[9] In contrast to state park use, campground use reached an all-time high, putting more pressure on the forest roads and inviting more criticism.[10]

And still the department leaders dreamed of increasing recreational use of the state lands. In December 1942 the Conservation Commission discussed establishment of a Green Trails system that would connect all parts of the state with trails for such activities as hiking, riding, and canoeing. Campgrounds and rest areas located every fifty miles or so would serve as stopping places. The idea was carried as far as Governor Murray D. Van Wagoner, who gave it his support but postponed implementation until after the war.[11] (Only now, in the early twenty-first century, is a modified version of this vision finally being realized.)

Even as the war continued, land became available for public purchase in tracts of various sizes owned by individuals and companies. These lands typically were heavily cut over and supported growth of aspen, pin cherry, and swamp conifers and often could be purchased for as little as two dollars an acre from owners who considered their property worthless and were delighted to get even such a low price.[12]

While many Michiganders viewed the cutover lands as worthless, many other observers saw the potential to once again grow valuable timber there. Changes were taking place on the land, and those changes were evident to those who took the time and effort to look for them.

IN 1939, THE FORESTRY DIVISION BEGAN TO STUDY THE RATE OF SPREAD of forest cover into openings resulting from fire, harvesting, and farming, and the study's results were released in 1942. The report concluded that

- the period of rapid natural closing in of old burned-over areas and abandoned farms was past;
- the rate and completeness with which openings closed since the initial spurt of sprouting and seeding following fires was affected by the soil type;
- most logged, unburned, hardwood areas returned rapidly to forest cover as a consequence of sprouting species and advanced reproduction occurring in the stand;
- where the timber was largely over mature, sprouting played little part in the restocking;
- where unburned cutover land had to restock by seeding, the process was slow but usually steady.
- the spread of forest cover into abandoned farmland was extremely slow and uncertain except where seeding took place soon after abandonment, before sod formed; much abandoned farmland in hardwood regions would probably remain open indefinitely;
- the presence of sod and other ground vegetation was the most important single factor in retarding the spread of forest cover into long-established openings.[13]

In the department's 1941–42 biennial report, Schaaf described the development of promising second-growth hardwoods in the northern Lower Peninsula and made recommendations for the management of those new stands. Timber sales were made on the Pigeon River Forest, with a ten-inch-diameter limit to remove scattered culls and remnants of the former stands. "Though three sections are included in the area, only small parts are put under permit at one time in order to allow a change in cutting specifications should the need arise."[14]

The Civilian Conservation Corps had thinned more than ten thousand acres of second-growth hardwoods across the state. The state custodians of these lands noted the potential of these young stands of timber and began a program of management that would guide them toward sustainable hardwood stands producing high-quality products. Schaaf remarked in 1944, "The increased demand for wood products and the high markets resulting from the war conditions have made it possible for this agency to make its maximum contribution to the effort and at the same time actually put our timber areas in better shape for future production."[15]

In 1942, the demand for timber from the state forests and game areas led the Conservation Commission to establish a list of minimum stumpage prices for state lands: sugar maple, red pine, and white pine sawtimber was priced at $6.00 per thousand board feet, while aspen pulpwood carried a minimum price of sixty-four cents per cord. Jack pine was a bit higher at $1.00 per cord, and spruce topped the list at $2.50 per cord.[16] "Stumpage" refers to the value of standing timber "on the stump."

Timber sales from the state forests in the 1940–41 fiscal year brought in $6,849; the following year, with the onset of the war, that amount nearly quadrupled to $25,860. The harvested volume in those two years was more than 2 million board feet of lumber and 17,500 cords of pulpwood and other miscellaneous products. In addition, more than four hundred thousand board feet of pine, hardwood, and tamarack plus assorted bridge timbers, pilings, table pieces, and other material was harvested for department use. Another 116 free use permits were issued so that local residents could obtain firewood.[17]

IN 1941–42, ALL OF THE LANDS UNDER JURISDICTION OF THE GAME DIVI-sion, known previously as "tracts," "public hunting grounds," "state game refuges," and "game areas," were reclassified as "game areas," and Game Division chief Harry Ruhl instituted a policy for their management: "The Division tries to achieve the best possible utilization of the land and its products through management programs drawn up annually for each district. Each game manager is in charge of all timber disposal and game management in his district and submits regular reports of game conditions which help the Department to formulate wise use policies and regulations affecting wildlife in the state as a whole." By 1942, the department had established twenty-three state game areas totaling more than 1.1 million acres.[18]

A program of timber sales was started on the game areas in 1940. Although the regulations permitted logging only when doing so would

☙ MARCUS SCHAAF, REGISTERED LAND SURVEYOR

Marcus Schaaf loved the Lake Superior State Forest and made many visits there, staying in one of the spare rooms at the headquarters. Schaaf was a registered land surveyor and he enjoyed getting his hands dirty during his visits, assistance that field
foresters welcomed.

On one such occasion, Schaaf was helping district forester Bernard McTiver with a
boundary line project when the chain they were using to measure the line suddenly
stopped moving. McTiver watched for a while and, seeing no movement of the chain,
went to see what had happened. He found the state forester in a most undignified
condition, climbing out of a shallow ravine and covered with smelly, black muck. He
had been attempting to cross the ravine on a log when the chain snagged, causing him
to lose his balance and fall in. The two resumed work and said nothing more about the
incident. The story was recounted many years later at Schaaf's retirement dinner, and
he delighted the crowd as he ended his retirement speech by announcing, "There's one
thing I still want to know—Bernie, did you or did you not snub that chain?"

improve timber stands for wildlife, virtually any treatment would have
qualified under that criterion. Nevertheless, the policy does not appear to
have been abused, as timber sale proposals submitted to the commission included approvals from the appropriate Fish Division and Field Administration (Fire and Law) Division supervisors and starting in March 1942 included
the district forester's signature as well.[19]

Game habitat conditions were changing somewhat on the state lands.
Deeryards were being improved by the increased timber harvest, meaning
that their habitat value would last longer than had originally been anticipated. However, as a consequence of starvation losses in the northeastern
Lower Peninsula, the deer population was no longer increasing.[20] By 1942,
the sharptail grouse had extended their range to within thirty miles of Sault
Ste. Marie, and biologists anticipated that all suitable habitat in the Upper
Peninsula soon would be stocked naturally. Efforts to establish sharptails in
the northern Lower Peninsula were continuing but were not yet considered
successful. The status of prairie chickens was reported as "changing": brush
and tree encroachment into their habitat resulted in declining numbers of
the birds in the western Upper Peninsula.[21]

IN JUNE 1944, HOFFMASTER BEGAN HIS PREFACE TO THE DEPARTMENT'S biennial report with the observation, "It behooves a people to keep watch over its resources and to take inventory of them once in a while." He continued, "The largest of our renewable resources is our forests. For 50 years or longer these forests were depleted faster than they were being replaced. When we were cutting as much as a county a year, and burning considerably more, we were losing. For over a half-century the trend was downward. But in the late '20s it started to change. It was then that the Legislature recognized forest fires as a devastating menace and by adequate appropriations made it possible to abate that menace. Appropriations have continued, public opinion has changed, and the trend has been upward." Also contributing to the change in the public perception of forests were the increasing uses being found for its products: in the past, "most of our timber was cut into saw logs and processed into lumber. If a tree wouldn't make lumber it was of no value. Today, we have masonite, and plywoods—products of cellulose, chemistry, the steam chest, and great presses—all substitutes for lumber. We are wondering if by cutting the crop younger—at 30 to 40 years instead of 75 to 150 years—we will not get much more from the land and have an even better product."[22]

The nature of the state forests had definitely changed, and so had their management. No longer was fire control the all-consuming priority. Timber was growing and it was time to start looking ahead. As Conservation Department managers looked forward, they saw the need for one administrative change that would give a final form to the state forest system over the next half century.

8

Postwar Development

1946–1958

In July 1946, Conservation Department director P. J. Hoffmaster noted that his agency was twenty-five years old and that it was time to evaluate its operation.[1] Four months earlier, on March 5, Hoffmaster had recommended to the Conservation Commission "that land management activities on northern forest and game area lands be placed in the hands of the Forestry Division." This move, he believed, would free Game Division personnel to do game management work and would simplify the public's understanding of division responsibilities.[2]

Hoffmaster began his March report with a review of the history of the two categories of state land. The state forests had started "about 1900" and included both tax-reverted lands and lands purchased with general funds through the $1.50 added to deer license fees. "It is interesting to note," he said, "that there is nearly as large an acreage of purchased land in the State

Forests as in the Game Areas"—the state forests had 200,000 acres of purchased land, while the game areas had 240,000 acres.[3]

In contrast, wrote Hoffmaster, "State Game Areas started about 1920 as State Game Refuges. By and large, these refuges were created from a nucleus of state homestead lands which were blocked in by purchase from game money, and by the addition of tax-reverted lands. Later, public hunting areas were set up around Game Refuges. About 1935, Game Refuges were abandoned and the Game Refuge–Public Hunting Ground Areas became Game Areas. Addition of tax-reverted lands since 1939 has greatly increased their size."[4]

Hoffmaster proposed that equal amounts of money be allocated from the General Fund and the Game Protection Fund, thereby symbolizing balance. He recognized that the "question might arise as to whether such a realignment of functions will reduce the effort devoted to game activities." He explained that he actually expected a gain in game management because the district foresters would spend about half their time on game-related duties. He also gave assurance of a balanced program, making it clear that, "such practices as planting, cutting, controlled burning, etc. cannot be put into effect by either the Forestry or Game Division without the concurrence of the other." All districts were to be called "forest-game areas."[5]

One member of the Conservation Commission, Joseph Rahilly of Newberry, disliked the name "forest-game areas" and suggested that the areas continue to be called "state forests." The public was familiar with the state forests as public hunting land, he said, and "the dictionary definition of 'forest' is sufficiently broad to cover the lands under consideration." With "state forests" inserted in place of "forest-game areas," the commission passed the recommendation.[6]

In a preface to the department's biennial report for 1945–46, Hoffmaster noted, "With the state forests a part of the Department, the forests have become more than acres for growing timber. They have been dedicated as public hunting grounds with game management practices carried on in accordance with recommendations of qualified men in the Game Division. Streams and lakes in the forests have the benefit of recommendations of trained people of the Fish and Fisheries Division. Park and Recreation Division employees have aided and advised in the construction and management of forest campgrounds, picnic sites, and other facilities."[7] With this

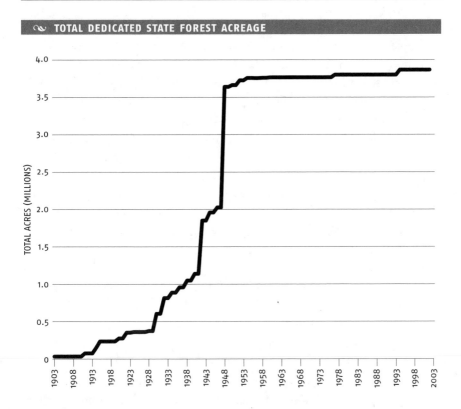

∾ TOTAL DEDICATED STATE FOREST ACREAGE

The substantial increase during and immediately following the Great Depression is due to thousands of acres reverting to the State for nonpayment of taxes. The increase that occurred in 1946 was a result of the Conservation Commission transferring state game lands in the northern two-thirds of the State to the administrative control of the Forestry Division.

description, the director defined a management philosophy that would come to be known as multiple use.

Hoffmaster directly addressed the shift in management of game areas. "One of the most far-reaching interdepartmental organization changes in the last decade was consummated during 1946 when administration of about 1,500,000 acres of northern Michigan lands in the so-called 'game areas' was shifted from the Game Division to the Forestry Division. Hitherto the forests and game areas were administered by the separate divisions, each carrying on much the same type of land use management. Under the present functional plan, actual administration of all dedicated wild lands, with some few exceptions, is under the Forestry Division with the game management activities on these lands directed by the Game Division."[8]

State Forester Marcus Schaaf put it this way: "On April 16, 1946, the Conservation Commission approved transfer of land management activities on Game Areas north of the Bay City–Muskegon line from the Game Division to the Forestry Division. The purpose of this change was to consolidate such activities under one division and to enable the field personnel of the Game Division to devote their entire energies to game management rather than to timber sales which had in many cases become the main part of their work. The plan will be put into effect July 1, 1946 after which time all Game Areas will become part of the State Forest system and will be known as State Forests."[9]

This action effectively doubled the size of the state forest system and set it on the path it was to follow for the next half century. The news of this decision hit like a bombshell among employees of both Game and Forestry Divisions. Forestry personnel received a strong vote of confidence and a big workload, while game officials were relieved of a lot of work but must have felt victimized. "There were some ruffled feathers," said Don Zettle, a Lansing staffer for Game Division at that time. "Game Division employees had a choice of whether to transfer with their forest to Forestry or stay with Game Division. Most left the forest and stayed with the Game Division."[10]

Many observers expressed skepticism about the plan. *Detroit Free Press* outdoor columnist Jack Van Coevering said, "As far as the State's sportsmen are concerned, they will measure the success of the proposed arrangements by the extent to which forest superintendents can broaden their thinking to cover wildlife needs as well as timber needs."[11] The Forestry Division had not convinced everyone of the breadth of its interests. Foresters took deep pride in the recovery of the forests under their custodianship, and this pride evidently spoke more loudly than the growing campground program and the other recreational developments in the state forests.

ONE MILESTONE FOR THE GROWING TIMBER RESOURCE WAS NOTED IN Schaaf's reference to the first commercial thinning of a state forest pine plantation in 1946. Although the location was not given, the statement described the stand as a twenty-nine-year-old stand containing mixed white pine and jack pine. Individual trees were marked for harvest, accounting for removal of 6.3 cords per acre and leaving 291 jack pines and 96 white pines per acre.[12] This effort represented a significant milestone: trees planted on barren, ravaged land had matured to the point that they had value, and the commercial thinning left the stand in better condition to grow in size, value, and beauty than before the harvest.

The availability of reliable timber operators was and remains a key factor in efficient management of the state forests. Timber sale policy was revised in January 1948 to help ensure the availability of operators of all sizes. The new policy established a small sale limit of two hundred dollars, twice the previous limit. This meant that any tract of timber to be offered for sale that had an estimated value of more than two hundred dollars must be offered at public auction. Forestry Division officials offered three reasons for the new policy:

1. It would accommodate and protect small operators and farmers who were less inclined or could not afford to bid for timber by making stumpage available to them in small amounts and on short notice.
2. It would attract larger operators by offering them sizable blocks of state timber.
3. Public auctions would enable equitable competition for the better pieces of timber.[13]

Beginning in 1951, sealed bids were permitted in special cases, and in 1954, sealed bids were officially added as an optional method, making them part of the standard procedure.[14]

THE FORESTERS WERE DOING THEIR JOB IN LOOKING AFTER THE VALUE OF the growing timber resource, but they were not blind to the other values of the forests. To provide life-sustaining browse for wintering deer, winter timber sales were emphasized within one mile of active deeryards. The Game Division asserted in 1960 that such sales had increased the carrying capacity of state deeryards by one hundred thousand deer.[15] In deeryard areas lacking commercial timber but needing additional food supplies, non-commercial cuttings were authorized. At first these cuttings were done by hand; beginning in the winter of 1958–59, a tree-shearing blade mounted on a large bulldozer came into use.[16]

Other lands were recognized for their scenic value or for certain unique vegetation or other characteristics: timber and game management did not always constitute the dominant value. Forest campgrounds were the first and most obvious of these lands with special values. The Jordan River Valley was recognized in the early 1950s as a special area and one in need of protection. A minimal development at the overlook called Deadman's Hill was designed to protect the site from overuse. The development restricted access and drew fire from local residents in 1952. The complaining delegation from Boyne City and the East Jordan Sportsmen's Club, the Ellsworth Sportsmen's Club, and others objected to the department's proposal for a picnic table, toilets, and parking area designed to keep traffic away from the overlook itself. They, too, wanted the site to be protected but differed with the department about how to do so.[17] The Department eventually provided minimum facilities at the popular site and protected the nearby environment.

The Michigan Natural Areas Council made recommendations for natural areas on state lands in the summer of 1954. These recommendations included establishment of four different use levels: natural area preserve, nature study area, scenic site, and nature reservation, each with detailed general rules. The recommendations were signed by the council's chair, Alexander H. Smith, and supported by Arthur Elmer, chief of the Parks and Recreation Division.[18] While there is no record that the commission formally adopted the council's recommendation, these designations were cited in the transfer of several square-mile sections from the Lake Superior State Forest to the Tahquamenon Falls State Park and the creation of the Betsy Lake Natural Area Preserve within the Lake Superior State Forest in August 1954.[19] Fossil beds were reserved on the Munuscong State Forest in June 1955, also at the recommendation of the Natural Areas Council. The state forests were growing up to be more than just timber.

WITH THE END OF WORLD WAR II, THE HIGGINS LAKE NURSERY WENT back into production, resuming the shipment of seedlings in the fall of

Higgins Lake State Forest Nursery, spring 1947. Post–World War II production was well under way. Courtesy of the Michigan Department of Natural Resources; photo by Russ Martin.

1946. That year, about 2.75 million seedlings were produced: all were sold to the public at the cost of production.[20] Reforestation on state land did not resume until 1949. This was the first planting to use the state's Reforestation Fund, established in 1945 using timber revenue from tax-reverted land.[21] With planting suspended during the war, the Reforestation Fund grew to around four hundred thousand dollars, and the department sought to allow the fund to continue to grow to a level that would cover the planting on state land of those seedlings intended for sale if the economy slowed and all the trees could not be sold to the private sector.[22]

The lack of available hand labor after the war changed the state's procedure for tree planting. In 1949–50, plantings were done "in areas prepared by scalping, by furrowing where only a shallow furrow was required, and by machines which, in addition to planting, also prepared the ground". Several commercial tree planters were purchased, and in addition this Division is

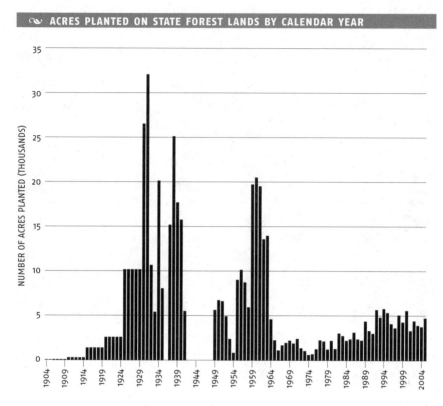

∞ ACRES PLANTED ON STATE FOREST LANDS BY CALENDAR YEAR

NUMBER OF ACRES PLANTED (THOUSANDS)

Besides hand and machine planting efforts, foresters also utilized direct seeding and scarification for natural regeneration.

developing a tree planting machine which will prepare areas by scalping [scraping away the sod mat] rather than furrowing and can be used to prepare land for hand planting crews or for planting by the machine itself."[23] By 1952, six of the planter/scalper machines (developed in part by future state forester Ted Daw) were in use.[24]

The Forestry Division leased the Wyman Nursery at Manistique from the U.S. Forest Service in 1950. The former Civilian Conservation Corps nursery had been idle for ten years, and its irrigation system needed major work, but its capacity was needed to feed the demand for seedlings on state and private lands. The Wyman and Higgins Lake nurseries together would have the capacity to produce 22 million seedlings annually.[25]

Hearty souls ride the mechanical tree planters reforesting the cutover abandoned lands that reverted to the state, circa 1955. Courtesy of the Michigan Department of Natural Resources.

In August 1953, the Conservation Commission endorsed a reforestation plan presented by the Forestry Division for both state and private lands. The plan called for planting trees on between 200,000 and 250,000 acres of state land and on 1.4 million acres of private open land plus 914,000 acres of private farmland. Seedling production at the state nurseries was to be increased to 28 million. The plan also suggested that the state grow sturdier stock to compete better with existing vegetation and give first priority in the allotment of planting stock to the needs of private landowners. In addition, the nursery program should be adjusted to meet private and state planting requirements, and lands primarily suited for forest production should be planted as fast as resources would permit. The plan also included allocations for more than 50 million seedlings among various government agencies and the private sector.[26]

Forestry efforts also received a boost in the mid-1950s from Governor G. Mennen Williams, a strong supporter of protection, management, and

Harvesting of nursery stock at the Higgins Lake State Forest Nursery, 1957. Courtesy of the Michigan Department of Natural Resources; photo by Clyde Allison.

reforestation of state lands who advocated expansion of the division's staff. In his 1954–55 budget message to the legislature, Williams noted that "proper management of our forests requires additional effort in surveying forest conditions and supervising cutting. Six additional foresters are included in the Conservation Department budget. Increased planting stock from the recently expanded Higgins Lake Nursery and other sources will be available for reforestation work in 1954–55. I am recommending funds sufficient to increase our state reforestation program from the current level of approximately 5 million trees annually to a planting program of 8 to 10 million trees in 1954–55." The following year, Williams stated in his budget message that he was "happy to report that because of past legislative approval of additional forester requests this division is becoming more nearly self-supporting through the survey of and sale of ripe timber." And again in his budget message for fiscal year 1956–57, Williams announced, "Reforestation of state lands will be stepped up to 20,000 acres and sufficient planting stock will be available to meet all private requests for seedlings."[27]

In Lansing, the Conservation Department's organization was becoming unwieldy with so much going on in the field so far away. To better respond to the situation, the department established regional offices in Marquette and Roscommon at the same time that the game areas were transferred.[28] On February 1, 1948, field activities were centered under regional chiefs in a department reorganization.[29]

The table on page 84 shows the twenty-one districts that emerged from the 1947 reorganization of Forestry and Game Division lands and their year of dedication. It also shows the influence of the Game Division—that is, of hunting license money—on state landownership in the Upper Peninsula. That Michigan acquired land in the Upper Peninsula can be directly attributed to Game Division Chief Harry Ruhl, whose foresight led to establishment of the northern game areas in spite of the belief among Forestry Division employees that these sites were too far from Lansing to be managed efficiently.

In September 1953, the Conservation Commission dedicated a tract of eighty-five acres in Van Buren County in southern Michigan as Fuller's Woods. The bulk of the tract consisted of eighty acres that Mortimer Fuller had donated to the state in 1938 for conservation purposes.[30] Today, Fuller's Woods is considered a part of the state forest system, the only southern Lower Michigan state forestland.

In July 1954, the 115,400-acre Michigamme State Forest was formed from parts of the Baraga, Sturgeon River, and Escanaba River State Forests. The commission had approved this change two years earlier, but the forest supervisor position was not funded until 1954. The commission minutes for July 1954 stated that "Clayton Schooley, assistant in the Houghton Lake District, was automatically certified to the new district forester job by the Civil Service Commission as he was first on the eligibility priority list due to his previous status at the district forester class. Mr. Schooley has already moved to Ishpeming," where the headquarters were to be established.[31]

The Forestry Division staff added a registered land surveyor in 1950, locating him near the northern tip of the Lower Peninsula. He was to work on running boundary lines and locating corners set by the Government Land

❧ FORESTRY DISTRICTS 1947

DISTRICT #	NAME	YEAR OF DEDICATION	FOUNDING DIVISION	ACRES OF STATE LAND
Region I (Upper Peninsula)				
1	Baraga	1946	Game	165,510
2	Iron Range	1942	Game	66,960
3	Sturgeon River	1930	Game	272,931
4	Escanaba River	1930	Game	191,606
5	Menominee	1940	Game	110,324
6	Grand Sable	1932	Game	197,028
7	Manistique River	1932	Game	160,508
8	Lake Superior	1913	Forestry	230,728
9	Mackinac	1928	Forestry	302,227
10	Munuscong	1925	Game	126,264
Region II (Northern Lower Peninsula)				
11	Hardwood	1928	Forestry	186,563
12	Black Lake	1928	Forestry	137,600
13	Pigeon River	1919	Forestry	129,240
14	Presque Isle	1915	Forestry	153,640
15	Alpena	1916	Forestry	77,120
16	Fife Lake	1913	Forestry	221,569
17	Au Sable	1928	Forestry	213,780
18	Higgins Lake	1903	Forestry	196,800
19	Pere Marquette	1935	Game	86,880
20	Houghton Lake	1903	Forestry	146,000
21	Ogemaw	1914	Forestry	229,440
Region III (Southern Lower Peninsula)				
22	Allegan	1940	Forestry	37,409

Source: Michigan Department of Conservation, Biennial Report, 1947–48, 125.

∽ SURVEYORS

Important survey corners such as that represented by this brass cap were reestablished throughout the public lands by state-employed registered land surveyors. The original survey took place from 1815 to 1853. Courtesy of the Michigan Department of Natural Resources; photo by LeRoy Stevens.

The Government Land Office (GLO) conducted a survey of most of Michigan in the 1840s. Work had begun some twenty years earlier in southeastern Michigan but had been suspended because of lack of interest in the land. The discovery of iron ore in the Upper Peninsula fueled a renewed interest in surveying. This GLO survey established the section, town, and range lines that form the basis for today's landownership. Wooden posts were set for the section corners and quarter-section corners and at least two "bearing trees" (BTs) were marked for each corner. Two axe blazes were made on each BT—one at breast height and one at the stump. On the upper blaze or "face" the section number was scribed; on the lower face the letters "BT" were scribed. Below the BT mark was a shallow notch. The distance and compass bearing from the corner post to the notch were recorded so that the corner location could be reestablished after the post had long since disappeared. Trees that happened to stand on the section lines were also blazed and recorded. Bearing trees and line trees were noted by their species and diameter. The surveyors' field notes are still on file in the county court houses and provide useful information. Even today, evidence from the original survey trumps work done with the most sophisticated modern instruments. Thus, finding "original evidence" is very significant.

Office survey a hundred years earlier.[32] Several district foresters were also registered surveyors, but they had minimal time available for surveying. A second full-time surveyor was added for the Upper Peninsula in 1958.[33]

In the 1964 reorganization, the surveyors were transferred from Forestry Division to a newly formed Engineering Division. However, the majority of their work remained with the state forests. During times of budget crisis, survey crews came under scrutiny and, at times, their existence seemed in jeopardy. In the 1980s they returned to Forest Management Division, where they remain.

IN APRIL 1957 A DEPARTMENT STUDY COMMITTEE RECOMMENDED TO THE Commission that the forest fire arm of the Field Administration Division be transferred to the Forestry Division. The study committee consisted of the three regional chiefs, Assistant Deputy Director Gaylord Walker, and the chiefs of Forestry and Field Administration. Regional Chief Aldrich and Field Administration Chief Robson dissented. The commission report explains: "Some Commission members had taken the position that the proposed transfer was a matter of 'policy,' with the making of which the Commission is charged by statute, rather than of 'administrative procedure'; Commission action during the April, 1957 meeting was sought to permit the change-over, if approved, with the start of the fiscal period beginning July 1, 1957." The state Senate had approved the transfer unanimously but then reversed itself the next day. Thus, the commission, rather than go against the wishes of the Senate, voted to defer the issue for at least a year.[34]

By 1947, Michigan's state forests covered an area equivalent to nearly three times the land area of the state of Delaware. Because of the great amount of land in each forest and the very small staff—generally one or two people—land managers often lacked familiarity with some parts of the forest. To remedy this situation, the Timber Management Survey (TMS) was begun in the spring of 1947. The effort was not meant to be a detailed survey but was intended merely "to give some indication of the present and future timber sale and planting possibilities." It was also meant to locate important game management areas, such as deeryards.[35]

James L. Halbach, district forester on the Mackinac State Forest during the years the TMS was under way, described his approach to the project: "I'd strap on my snowshoes early in the morning and I'd start into the woods . . . taking notes and mapping as I went. I'd go as far as I could until lunch time. Then I'd move over a quarter mile and return on a parallel line, still taking notes and mapping."[36] Notes were kept in pocket-sized field books, and maps at a scale of four inches to the mile were sketched inside. Stands were classified into five cutting periods according to their age and condition, while stocking levels were expressed in three levels. In addition, mappers recorded diameter ranges for the trees in each stand.

Sometimes during the land examination connected with the timber management survey or in the course of other management activities, foresters came across cabins built on state lands. Such cabins were termed "trespass cabins" and were of various sizes and construction. They ranged from solid, old log structures to tarpaper shacks. Some had existed since before the land became part of the state forest; others were constructed in defiance of state ownership. All were illegal, and foresters attempted to contact the "owners" of these cabins to get them removed from state land.

Officials usually found some way to identify and contact the occupants of the trespass cabins—often by visiting during deer hunting season. Foresters then arranged to have the cabin moved or dismantled; in a few cases, when honest attempts to survey the land had been made, the state exchanged land with the cabin owner. In some instances, however, no contact could be established, and foresters would leave notes in or on the cabins giving instructions to contact the Forestry Division or the cabin would be destroyed.

The foresters came up with many creative ways to destroy the structures, but records were not kept and those who know are reluctant to tell. One former district forester developed a healthy respect for the strength of the traditional log cabin as he attempted to pull one apart with a "come-along" winch. Foresters did not particularly enjoy this part of their job, but the existence of private camps on public lands was inconsistent with the purpose and policies of those lands, and the structures had to be removed to discourage an increase in their numbers.

The TMS provided a systematic way for the foresters to get out and see timber stands and evaluate their condition. The amount of effort invested in the survey varied with the individual district forester's workload and interest and with the accessibility of the land. By June 1952, half of the state forest system had been visited and mapped under this program.[37] Four years later, the survey was 72 percent complete; in 1958, 73 percent. The department's 1960 biennial report failed to mention the TMS.[38]

Preceding the start of the TMS by a few months was a cooperative program between the state and federal governments to make a statistical survey of Michigan's forest resources. The Lake States Forest Experiment Station launched the Lake States Forest Inventory in the fall of 1946 with the goal of producing a report on the volume and condition of Michigan's forests of all ownerships.[39] The effort was scheduled for completion in 1955, but personnel changes caused setbacks: fieldwork continued through the spring of 1956, and the publications were not finished until 1958.[40] When it was finally completed, the Michigan Forest Survey was hailed as "the greatest accumulation of information on Michigan forests ever done."[41]

In March 1949, Marcus Schaaf retired after thirty-nine years as state forester. He had started out with an office at Higgins Lake and a state forest system of about thirty thousand acres and had overseen incredible change and growth so that at his departure, the forester had a much larger office in Lansing and a system that included more than 3.5 million acres.

Schaaf was replaced by his former assistant, George S. McIntire. After a couple of years as state forester, in 1952, McIntire assessed the division's function, focusing particularly on expanded timber management. Sales were up by 58 percent over the previous biennium, and officials needed more specific knowledge about the existing forests and more technical knowledge regarding how to manage them. In addition, private forestry assistance was now a part of every district forester's job. Landowners could call district foresters to receive help with land-management issues. Nurseries also constituted an important part of the Forestry Division program, as did special surveys such as the TMS, forest pest detection, and many other projects.[42]

In addition to the good information being gathered by the TMS and the Michigan Forest Survey, state forestry operations needed hard data on state-owned timber resources, which were clearly growing and becoming a subject of interest to more and more forest industries. Not wishing to repeat the pattern of exploitation from which the lands were recovering, the Forestry Division, with help from the U.S. Forest Service regional office in Milwaukee, began yet another inventory project in 1950. This one, called the Continuous Forest Inventory (CFI), was based on establishment of one-fifth-acre permanent plots randomly placed throughout the state forests. Measurements of all trees on the plots were taken when the plots were set up, with remeasurements to be made at five-year intervals. The sample plots would give a good estimate of the current volume of timber,

∿ A DAY IN DEADSTREAM

Retired district forester Jack Lockwood recalled working on the CFI at the Deadstream Swamp west of Houghton Lake with partner Peter Grieves.

It was a very warm and humid day. . . . This was to be the first remeasurement since the plots were established and the trees first measured. The lucky guys who put in these particular plots were Bob Borak and Ed Ecker. . . . We had Bob and Ed's notes, which described the location of the strip and how to get to it. We could see that this was going to be a long slog through the swamp just to find the strip. In addition to the description of bearings and distances that we were to follow, it was standard practice for crews to occasionally paint-mark trees along the route to add confidence to our compassing and pacing.

Right from the start we were in a dense stand of tag alder and ankle-deep water with clouds of mosquitoes for company. Those conditions, along with the oppressive heat, made it difficult to run an accurate line. So the farther we went, the more we relied on the paint marks from years ago to keep us on course. But, often the only "trees" available to mark were spindly alder stems, and the paint tended not to stick to the alder bark very well, especially after five years. We spent a lot of time sloshing about searching for the merest tiny flake of paint to tell us we were still on track.

I've forgotten how far we progressed in this manner, but I do remember getting very discouraged and even thinking we might never find the damn strip when ahead there appears a huge, very old, white pine stump blackened by countless fires, and there, on the stump, in perfectly preserved white paint were the words "Are you still with us, boys?"

With that uplift of our spirits, we went on to find the strip, measure what few trees were there, and make our way back to high ground.

while the periodic remeasurement of the same trees would track their growth and other changes.

Forestry students or recent graduates were hired to do the CFI fieldwork. Many career foresters began their professional experience in this way. Youth, with its optimism and stamina, may have been an important factor here, as the establishment of CFI plots was rigorous work. Two-person crews carried a supply of metal plot stakes (used to mark the center of each plot), data punch cards, measuring devices, marking paint, and their lunch as they compassed a line into the woods to where the plots had been randomly specified. White paint was squeezed from a tube to write "CFI" and an arrow on a tree where the compass line left the road and to number and mark the trees in the plots.

By June 1954, CFI work had been completed on nine forests in the northern Lower Peninsula, and work was beginning in the Upper Peninsula. Two forests in the northern Lower Peninsula were considered to be too scattered in their ownership pattern to produce reliable data. As Forestry Division officials looked at the initial data from the Lower Peninsula forests in 1957–58, they saw strong indications that harvest should be higher to maintain the desired forest health conditions. The aspen harvest needed to be doubled.[43]

At the same time as the various forest surveys were taking place, the state forests' normal day-to-day activities continued. In addition to reforestation, the creation and maintenance of campgrounds, and the management of timber sales, foresters faced a constant demand for permits of various kinds, including use permits (for long-term uses such as grazing and farming), special use permits (for rifle and archery ranges, landing fields, field trials, boat liveries, and other such activities); road access permits (requests to build roads across state land to gain access to private lands); free timber permits (primarily for firewood for home use, fence posts, or the like); mineral permits (gravel for county road commissions, department roads, and other projects); and building removal (for the sale and removal of surplus buildings).

Tending to the well-being of the growing forests became more complicated as they developed. In the early years, tree planting and fire protection constituted the primary concerns, but as the mosaic of forest cover began to gain maturity and diversity, more attention needed to be given to insects and diseases that could cause serious damage. In the spring of 1950, the Forestry Division initiated the Forest Pest Detection Program in cooperation with the U.S. Forest Service, Michigan State College, the University of Michigan, and the Michigan Department of Agriculture. The program sought to stop outbreaks of forest insects and diseases, facilitate and organize direct control in emergencies, and provide a basis for desirable protective measures.[44]

In 1951, the division added to its staff a forest entomologist, whose duties included monitoring of jack pine budworm, forest tent caterpillar, oak wilt, red-headed pine sawfly, European pine sawfly, European pine shoot moth, Saratoga spittlebug, pine spittlebug, larch casebearer, larch sawfly, and white pine weevil. Certain areas considered high-risk for these pests were included in a system of observation plots to be examined periodically by the district foresters. Dutch elm disease was also being noticed in the Detroit area.[45]

The forest tent caterpillar defoliated about a million acres in 1952 and 1.4 million acres in 1953 but declined in 1954.[46] The department's policy for controlling outbreaks recognized the natural tendency toward population collapse after a relatively short time and called for intervention only where extensive tree mortality was anticipated.

Action was taken against the Saratoga spittlebug in the 1953–54 biennium, with a 400-acre aerial spray program on the Thunder Bay River State Forest, but such actions were not common.[47] Mortality rates of 10–15 percent were noted in red and jack pine in northwest Lower Michigan in 1958, but chemical intervention was not deemed necessary. However, Saratoga spittlebug was targeted again in 1959, when 558 acres were sprayed with DDT and the "plantations made excellent recovery."[48]

Foresters were also concerned with silviculture—that is, with determining how best to manipulate the forest cover to keep trees healthy. Work was well under way to develop guidelines for management of northern hardwoods, but many questions remained concerning the management of the other forest types, which had received little attention. Research projects were established to look at numerous topics—for example, red pine thinning, jack pine disking, jack pine seed source, deer browse, aspen management, swamp reproduction, and many more.[49] Perhaps the best known of these early projects was the red pine thinning study begun in 1950 on a plantation established in 1913 on an old potato field near Higgins Lake. This study was intended to help determine what spacing of trees or number of trees per acre would result in the best growth. Known as the Bosom Field plantation after former farmer/owner Charles Bosom, this stand was a part of the research that established management recommendations for red pine plantations across the lake states.[50]

Managing jack pine stands drew the attention of both researchers and field foresters, who recognized that some sites were best suited for jack pine because of their droughty conditions and low fertility. Although jack pine had generally been used as a filler in red and white pine stands with the intention of removing it in the first thinning, some plantations of pure jack pine were started in the 1950s.[51] The division purchased two heavy-duty disks so that disking could be undertaken for jack pine regeneration, thereby providing a bare mineral soil seedbed by scraping away competing vegetation. Disking was done both before and after harvest of jack pine in hopes that the cones in the tops of the trees would release their seeds onto the freshly prepared sites.[52]

Deer exclosures were set out on state lands across the state to determine the effects of the growing deer herd (estimated at 1 million animals in 1950) on forest reproduction.[53] Studies were initiated to learn about aspen sprouting following cutting or burning. Disking was attempted as a means to increase the number of sprouts per acre in sparse stands. Initially, the disking did result in more trees per acre than were in the original stand, but their vigor was reduced by the chopping of the roots into short lengths. In the end, the stands looked very much like their predecessors.[54]

Many other trials and studies were installed to allow the department to better manage its state forests. In most cases, silvicultural trials and studies require at least several years for results to become evident. Hardwood thinning, which was begun experimentally by the Civilian Conservation Corps in the 1930s, became an accepted practice in the 1940s, as is apparent from the change in cutting specifications on state timber sales approved by the Conservation Commission. Until September 1947, specifications were for removal of trees of a given species above a certain diameter. That month, however, saw the first recorded hardwood sale involving only marked trees. It was on the Escanaba River State Forest and carried these specifications: "Only the hardwoods and hemlock marked for cutting will be removed." Other such marked sales soon followed.[55]

The first timber marking for harvest occurred in 1947. At first, axes with the letter S on the poll, or back edge of the head, were used. The bark on selected trees was chopped off down to bare wood in a spot about chest or eye level, and then the back of the axe was swung into the tree, stamping the S into the exposed wood. For obvious reasons, this system posed considerable danger to the person doing the marking. In the 1950s, paint guns became the normal tool for marking trees. Occasional questions have arisen about the relative safety of marking paint, but tests have proven it quite safe—much more so than axes.

In the 1930s and 1940s the research arm of the U.S. Forest Service at the Dukes Forest Experiment Station in Marquette County developed rules for marking hardwood timber under a silvicultural system known as individual tree selection. This system has proven very effective in guiding northern hardwood stands back to conditions similar to the old growth that existed in the nineteenth century.

Much has been said about the importance and prevalence of professionally trained foresters in the development and advancement of the state forest system. Another class of employees that contributed a great deal to the success of the state forests was the forestry aides (later known as forest technicians).

The technicians were not professionally trained but brought a wealth of practical experience to the job. Some had been loggers, some had been farmers, while others came from a wide variety of other backgrounds. They knew how to maintain equipment and received enough on-the-job training to be experts at timber cruising, scaling, and surveying.

Technicians typically were put in charge of tree planting operations and campground construction as well as numerous timber management tasks. They generally were assigned to a given area long enough to become thoroughly familiar with the terrain, ownership pattern, local timber jobbers, and other characteristics. For this reason, many area foresters considered them more valuable than professional foresters.

A TOPIC OF DEBATE FROM THE TIME OF THE 1946 DEPARTMENTAL REORGANIZATION was the treatment of the remaining forest openings. Game enthusiasts were concerned about the future of habitat for sharptail grouse and prairie chickens as the forests gradually reclaimed these openings. Pine plantations were anathema to biologists and others who favored the open spaces. Because of the lack of habitat-forming undergrowth in well-stocked pine plantations, biologists referred to them as "wildlife or biological deserts." Foresters often believed that too much land would be required in openings to justify widespread management for the prairie birds, which were not native to Michigan and served as a reminder of the extent of the deforestation that had occurred.

In 1950, while stocking efforts were still under way in the northern Lower Peninsula to successfully establish a sustainable population of sharptails,[56] foresters and game biologists sat down with maps and worked out plans for the forest openings. These Area Plan Maps were intended to resolve the problems regarding the planting of openings. No doubt they did help, but disagreements continued just the same. "I cannot reconcile good land use with the high percentage of plantable area withheld for a single game species," a district forester wrote.[57] "I received your tree planting forms today, and am returning twelve unsigned and signing one," a game biologist replied.[58] A district forester wrote to his regional supervisor, "In working up planting plans for the fall of 1961, we have hit a rather severe obstruction which we must handle before we can proceed."[59] Despite their imperfections, the Area Plan Maps served for about fifteen years and provided some basis for reason and discussion.

Controlled burns, mostly to reduce the amount of trees and brush encroaching on the open habitat for sharptails and prairie chickens, became a part of state forest management around 1950.[60] Aerial application of herbicides was tried with good results in 1954.[61]

An organization such as the Conservation Department starts with a general operational policy and adds additional policies as the need arises. Such a need arose in 1952, when Homer Peake, a timber jobber from Trout Lake, charged that Francis P. "Pat" Furlong, a former Conservation Department Field Administration Division district supervisor, had extorted money on a timber deal. Furlong had a pulpwood brokerage business that caused a possible conflict of interest with his job in the Conservation Department, although he had been retired from that job for eighteen months when the charges were filed.[62]

An investigation took place to determine whether Furlong's Conservation Department position had led to undue influence on state timber harvest. Stanley G. Fontana, a former deputy director for the Conservation Department and at the time the dean of the School of Forestry at the University of Michigan, conducted the investigation, which concluded, "We found plenty of evidence that Furlong was engaged in the timber business, but no evidence that he had cut on state lands."[63] Fontana went on to say that conservation officers under Furlong's supervision had gone into the logging business and that this had been a topic of discussion at many Conservation Department staff meetings. He blamed Conservation Commissioner Joseph Rahilly for supporting Furlong and thus condoning the involvement of Field Administration employees in outside businesses. In contrast to the Field Administration Division procedures, State Forester McIntire prohibited Forestry Division personnel from taking outside jobs of any kind, leading to dissension among department employees who resented the differing treatment. An erosion of public respect clearly had occurred in areas where the activities in question were taking place.[64]

Other parties joined in the fray, with public criticism coming from the Cleveland-Cliffs Iron Company, which owned and managed a large block of land in the Newberry area.[65] Paul A. Herbert, director of conservation at Michigan State College, suggested that "some Commissioners were assuming too much of an administrative function," and Volmar J. Miller, president of the Michigan United Conservation Clubs, added, "For some time we have heard [similar] rumors and reports . . . and it has become evident in the Upper Peninsula that there has been an increasing disrespect in recent years for Conservation Department personnel and the administration of conservation affairs due to the conduct of department personnel and their superiors."[66]

As evidence of the erosion of trust, a timber trespass on state forest land in the Black Lake State Forest made the front page of the *Detroit Free Press* and launched an attorney general's investigation of whether the local conservation officers had known about the trespass before it was publicly reported.[67] The department's image and ability to function were at stake; new policies clearly needed to be established.

In January 1953, the director of the Department of Conservation, Gerald E. Eddy, reported to the commission on the results of a survey of all department employees' outside employment: 335 employees had outside jobs of fifty different types that fell into three categories: (1) not allied with department work (e.g., farming, trades, clerical); (2) marginal (e.g., selling Christmas trees, writing, trucking, landscaping, fisheries consultant, real estate, photo and art, radio and TV repair); and (3) similar to department function (e.g., trapping, timber operations, guiding, sale of bait minnows).[68]

At its February 1953 meeting, the Conservation Commission adopted a new policy: "Employees of the Department shall not engage in any activity for monetary gain when that activity is allied with the conservation field if: (1) so doing will interfere with his regular duties; (2) such activity might discredit the employee or result in justifiable criticism of the Department."[69]

Over the next fifty years a variety of other laws, rules, regulations, and court decisions have dealt with similar issues. Indeed, in 2003 the Michigan Civil Service Commission adopted a revised rule for all state employees that provides, in part, that an employee shall not "engage in supplemental employment that conflicts with the satisfactory or impartial performance of the employee's state duties." These rules require express written consent from the agency before an employee can engage in supplemental employment.[70]

In 1950 the state forest system included about 85 campgrounds and provided camping opportunities for an estimated 75,000–100,000 people annually.[71] Use of the campgrounds increased steadily, surpassing 400,000 in 1960, when there were 105 campgrounds in the system.[72]

In 1958 the state outlined a program of "total use" for the state forests. This program was aimed at integrating public uses into the general forest area by installing interpretive signs identifying such actions as areas planted, harvested, or burned for blueberry production or sharptail habitat. Marked trails and scenic drives were a part of the program, as was a goal of doubling the number of campgrounds.[73] Remnants of this program are visible throughout northern Michigan. Reforestation work continued rapidly through the 1950s, covering a total of nearly seventy-five thousand acres on state lands with 60 million trees planted in the decade.[74] Demand for planting stock for private lands also remained strong, and the department adopted a policy of providing trees to fill those needs first.[75] Addition of the Wyman nursery did not bring total production up to the level needed to fill the demand. The Hardwood Nursery reduced its selection of species from forty-three to twenty in 1952 in an attempt to increase efficiency and cut costs and in 1956 changed its production to two-thirds conifers in a further effort to reduce costs per unit and fill the gap in conifer production.[76]

In September 1956, the Conservation Commission authorized Eddy to enter into agreements with the U.S. Forest Service that would meet the state's obligations under the federal Soil Bank and Agricultural Conservation Programs, established under the Agricultural Act of 1956. This meant even more tree planting. A 50/50 state-federal match would be provided for planting on public lands, with a 40/40/20 match on private lands, with the 20 percent supplied by the owner. Other state obligations included an additional nursery, technical assistance to landowners, and facilitating game management.[77]

The commission approved a site between Brighton and Pinckney in Livingston County for the new nursery and authorized purchase of the land in December 1956.[78] Construction began in 1958, and a limited number of trees was shipped in 1960.[79] Production from the new Southern Michigan Nursery went in part to replace that produced by two Michigan State University nurseries closed in 1960.[80]

Planting was done by machine almost exclusively throughout the 1950s, with fifty-seven planting machines, known as killifers, in service in 1956.[81] More than a dozen of these machines were equipped with a foot-operated sprayer that could be used to squirt a small amount of a pesticide, aldrin, on the roots of the seedlings just before they were put into the ground.[82] The pesticide was used to control depredations by white grubs, the larvae of the large june beetle or june bug and reduced tree mortality rates from 40 percent to 6 percent. Many of the sodded planting sites were heavily infested with these grubs, which often would lie exposed on the freshly scalped furrow behind the planting machine. Flocks of blackbirds could be seen walking the furrows behind the planters, gobbling up the white grubs.[83] The U.S. Environmental Protection Agency banned aldrin for most uses in 1974 and totally banned the product in 1987. It is classified as a probable human carcinogen and is no longer produced in or imported into the United States.

As the state forest system passed the half century mark, both the agency and the forest were maturing. As a consequence of cost considerations and of the often isolated locations of the forest headquarters, they were gradually eliminated. In 1950 the Grand Sable headquarters in Schoolcraft County became the summer camp for the University of Michigan Department of Geography, and the Sturgeon River headquarters in Dickinson County was deeded to Nadeau Township Schools for use as an outdoor education center.[84] The trout-rearing station on the Otter River in the Baraga State Forest was given to Michigan College of Mining and Technology in 1955 to be used for forestry and wildlife management education.[85] Other buildings were sold and dismantled or moved as district offices were opened in nearby towns.

McIntire noted this forest maturation and recovery in 1958: "Michigan's state forests, with 20 percent of the forest land of the state, are now producing approximately 20 percent of the total pulpwood harvested in the State. This represents a milestone in the long climb from non-productive, cut-over, burned-over, barren land of a half-century ago to forests contributing their proportionate share of a major segment of the State's wood requirements. It is significant in view of the tremendous simultaneous increase in the use of these same lands for hunting, fishing, camping, touring and other forms of recreation and outdoor enjoyment."[86]

And so Michigan's state forests and the Forestry Division looked forward to the new challenges that lay ahead.

9

The Fully Managed, Multiple-Use Forest Era

1959–1975

GEORGE S. MCINTIRE RETIRED IN JANUARY 1961, HAVING SERVED AS CHIEF of the Forestry Division for almost twelve years. Conservation Department Director Gerald Eddy commended McIntire for his support and encouragement of the multiple-use concept and appointed Theron E. "Ted" Daw as McIntire's successor, only the third state forester in fifty-one years. Daw was a forestry graduate of Michigan Agricultural College and had been a division employee for more than thirty years.[1] Observers anticipated little change in direction with Daw's assumption of the division's leadership, as noted in Conservation Commission proceedings: "Mr. Daw, on the invitation of [Commissioner Robert F.] Brevitz, sketched briefly his career in the Department since June 17, 1929, under his 'immediate supervisor,' Mr. McIntire, that relationship having continued through the years, declaring that with such indoctrination he could only carry on with the latter's concepts and principles."[2]

State Forester George McIntire (left) and Assistant State Forester Ted Daw admire this framed photo donated to the Michigan Conservation Commission by Mrs. A. A. Crego of Trout Lake in 1959. The framed photo was taken in the spring of 1905 by Monte Laur of Gaylord and depicts some of the last virgin white pine in Michigan that stood on the David Ward Estate in Antrim County. Courtesy of the Michigan Department of Natural Resources.

Daw took over as chief of the Forestry Division at a time of austerity. Nursery stock sales were down 20 percent, and timber revenue had dropped from $755,000 in fiscal 1961 to $679,000 in 1962.[3] The budget was so tight that the department's biennial report for 1961–62 was typewritten rather than published commercially. Even though the revenue picture was bleak, considerable attention was paid to the state forests as a consequence of their recreational potential. In August 1961, Governor John D. Swainson charged the Conservation Commission with coordinating the recreation programs of all the state agencies. The commission was happy to accept this responsibility and to see the emphasis on recreation.[4] In October 1961, the commission made several recommendations, including an inventory of current services and projected needs and the establishment of a Recreation Unit in the Conservation Department with a deputy director for recreation.[5]

In spite of the austerity of the time, Forestry Division officials had noted an increase in recreational use. To balance the workload for the year, a sign shop was established at the Southern Michigan Nursery to be active primarily in the winter months, when nursery work was slow. The department started five educational and scenic forest drives and developed ten small campgrounds in the 1961–62 biennium.[6] Multiple-use maps were developed to guide management for timber, game, and recreation. These maps also designated certain special use areas.

As a result of the deliberations on recreational development, significant state forest lands and campgrounds were transferred to the Parks Division to become a part of that system. These included St. Vital Point (Munuscong State Forest) to DeTour State Park (268 acres); Duncan Bay (Black Lake State

Interpretive signs were placed throughout the state forest system during the 1960s and 1970s. The routed, rustic signs were produced at the nurseries, often with prison labor. The pine lumber was cut from state forestlands. Courtesy of the Michigan Department of Natural Resources.

Forest) to Cheboygan State Park (498 acres); and a portion of the Fife Lake State Forest to Benzie State Park (2,037 acres).[7]

By 1962, the number of state forest campgrounds had grown to 112. Some received very heavy use—enough to cause concern that rules and regulations (particularly the twenty-day maximum stay rule) were not being followed. The division implemented a tag system on these campgrounds to improve compliance with the twenty-day rule.[8]

In 1965, snowmobile trails were added to the recreational opportunities on the state forests. Snowmobiles were relatively new, and forestry personnel lacked a good understanding of what would constitute attractive recreational trails for the vehicles. Assuming that most snowmobilers would enjoy seeing some areas that were nearly inaccessible at other times of year, the staffs laid out trails in scenic but remote areas. Layout and trail marking took a lot of time and public use of the early trails was disappointing.

A second factor drawing attention to the state forests was a study done in cooperation with Michigan State University on the economic contributions of the state forests. The study showed that timber ranked first (contributing 69 percent of the revenue raised by state forests), followed by hunting (14 percent), fishing (9 percent), oil and gas production (6 percent), and camping (2 percent). The study also found that "one dollar's worth of stumpage sold from the state forests resulted in $62 in wages, salaries, and profits, and $80 in total product value ready for the consumer."[9]

REFORESTATION DECLINED IN THE 1960S AS GOALS WERE REDUCED FROM twenty thousand acres per year to ten thousand acres in 1960 and to five thousand shortly thereafter. The reforestation of the state forestlands was finally being accomplished. Sites in need of planting were becoming harder to find, and improvement work on existing stands was rated as a better investment. The statewide austerity had led to a depletion of the reforestation fund, and labor was in short supply. A small planting program was deemed necessary to maintain a "safety valve" to use up surplus nursery stock if need be.[10]

The state Hardwood Nursery near Wolverine that had been established in 1935 was closed in 1962 because "experience with [hardwood] plantings in northern Michigan indicated the futility of attempting to establish hardwoods artificially, particularly where there were heavy concentrations of deer. This type of stock is still needed in farm-game planting programs in southern Michigan, and its production has been transferred to the new [Southern Michigan] nursery."[11]

DEER BROWSING REMAINED A CONCERN ACROSS THE NORTHERN TWO-thirds of the state. A study of the Ottawa National Forest in the western Upper Peninsula showed severe impacts. Measurements in 1953, 1955, 1958, and 1961 concluded that sugar maple was coming through, although damaged. However, the study continued, "hemlock, yellow birch and basswood have fared very poorly and apparently will be very scarce in future stands."[12]

The state's deer herd was a topic of hot discussion. Biologists were desperately trying to bring the herd's population down to within the natural carrying capacity of the range. This meant killing antlerless deer (does), an unpopular idea with sportsmen. The early conservation philosophy that called for hunters' restraint to build up the herd had taken root and refused to die. In July 1962, the Conservation Commission recorded "many complaints on the 'doe season.'"[13]

Gathering less attention but nonetheless important was the attempt to improve deer habitat. In the early 1960s, more than one thousand acres were being treated annually on the state forests with tree-cutting blades mounted on large bulldozers.[14] Typically, areas of aspen of mixed ages and intermixed with pine or other species were treated with this equipment to "set back the [forest] succession" and create thick stands of aspen sprouts, which form important habitat for deer. Controlled burns and aerial spray were also used to prevent tree cover from taking over important openings. These latter treatments were intended to maintain habitat as much for sharptail grouse as for deer, but they helped deer habitat as well.[15]

Sportsmen sometimes complained about the planting of red pine on state lands. In 1961, the Otsego County Chamber of Commerce went on record in opposition to further "excessive" red pine planting because of its negative effects on deer habitat.[16] The chamber members perhaps were unaware that a reduction in pine planting had already taken place and that the entire planting program since its inception had affected only about 2 percent of state forestland. But the red pine issue would not soon go away.

FORESTERS ALSO CONTINUED TO SEARCH FOR WAYS TO RESTORE FOREST cover to the former pineries, many of which remained grassland studded with pine stumps. One area on which reforestation efforts had failed straddled the line between Luce and Schoolcraft Counties in the eastern Upper Peninsula. Known as the Danaher Plains, after the company that logged it in the nineteenth century, this area covered perhaps twenty thousand acres between the upper reaches of the Tahquamenon and Fox Rivers. Large white pine stumps indicated that the site was good enough to support pine, but red pines planted there looked decidedly unhappy. Few trees survived, and those that did so were stunted and unhealthy-looking.

Reforestation efforts began on the Danaher Plains in the 1950s with red pine, which has a lower nutrient requirement than white pine and was deemed better suited to the now harsh, droughty conditions. Half a century after the white pine was cut, the only cover was a mixture of sedge grass and reindeer moss with an occasional serviceberry bush. The prominent feature of the landscape was the stumps.

Red pine did not fare well on the plains, however: survival rates were poor, and those trees that did survive grew slowly and without vigor. Some soil impoverishment resulting from the intense fires was the suspected culprit, but no particular nutrient was identified as lacking.

A cooperative project with Michigan State University begun in 1961 aimed to find ways to establish trees on such sites.[17] Project employees tested jack pine, which has a lower nutrient requirement than red or white pine, by planting it on the Luce County portion of the plains. The jack pine did remarkably well.

Plant pathologist Dr. Johann Bruhn from Michigan Technological University became interested in the situation in the 1980s and took a look at the mycorrhizal fungi (which assist trees in extracting minerals from the soil) on the roots of the pines. The project was never finished, however. Studies elsewhere have shown that the lichen (reindeer moss) that covers much of the ground on the plains has a negative effect on the establishment of soil fungi and soil moisture.

The Conservation Department initiated a later study in cooperation with Michigan State University to test various species and methods of site preparation, but all the trees in this experiment died. Dr. Robert Heyd, forest health specialist with the Michigan Department of Natural Resources in Marquette, had the soil tested for herbicides, and the results showed picloram, a chemical that wildlife managers commonly used at that time to kill invading trees to maintain openings. No one claimed responsibility for killing the trees.

The red pines that struggled for a foothold have finally become well established and are now growing vigorously. Stands are being thinned commercially, producing pine lumber from the plains once again. The exact cause of the problems with pine establishment on the plains remains a mystery, but time has made this question moot. With Mother Nature's persistence and a little help from the foresters, the pineries are being restored on the Danaher Plains.

THE SLOW ECONOMY OF THE EARLY 1960S LED COMMISSIONER MATT Laitala of Hancock to suggest that people could be put to work on the state forests in the Upper Peninsula. Daw responded at the October 1962 Conservation Commission meeting that recent changes in the Reforestation Act made it possible to use timber revenue for timber stand improvement as well as reforestation.[18] Revenues were going up, yet the need for reforestation was declining. This fund gradually would cover more and more of the state forests' management activities.

EARLY IN 1964, DR. RALPH A. MACMULLAN, A WILDLIFE RESEARCH BIOlogist, was appointed to succeed Eddy as director of the Conservation Department. One of his first actions was to move administrative power within the department to the field. Three deputy directors were named in Lansing: Dorias Curry, in charge of the field; Charles D. Harris, in charge of staff; and Gaylord A. Walker, in charge of services. Accompanying this move was the appointment of three regional managers: Glenn C. Gregg in Region I (Upper Peninsula), C. Troy Yoder in Region II (northern Lower Peninsula), and Warren Shapton in Region III (southern Lower Michigan).[19] This organizational change was implemented to help administrators be more responsive to needs in the field, but it also had the long-term effect of enhancing cooperation among divisions in the field.

MacMullan commented on the Conservation Department's overall condition in his portion of the department's 1963–64 biennial report: "Ten years of enforced austerity have left the Department inadequately staffed and seriously under-financed. Recruitment of young, vigorous people to supplement the existing force of loyal, seasoned employees is essential."[20]

Changes were made later at lower levels in the department that had a more direct effect on the Forestry Division and the state forests. In 1965, the Forest Fire Division was split from Law Enforcement. District offices were shuffled around in an attempt to make the division structures more nearly parallel. Forestry had twenty-two districts, while the other divisions had far fewer. The result was formation of four large districts in Region I (Baraga, Crystal Falls, Escanaba, and Newberry) and four in Region II (Gaylord, Mio, Gladwin, and Cadillac). Most divisions were represented by district supervisors.[21] Forestry was represented in all but Crystal Falls.

This shuffling of districts created a problem for the Forestry Division. Certain district foresters, who had been in charge of state forests, were promoted to the new positions, but their titles and salaries remained the same, pending review by the Civil Service Commission. And since it did not make sense to have two different positions with the title "district forester," those in charge of the state forests became known as "area foresters." This change seemed logical until the salary question came up. The title "area" indicated something lower than a "district," so the pay rate was lowered for the state forest positions. When the Civil Service Commission completed its study, the new district forester position was upgraded, but area forester remained at its lower level. Many foresters were insulted by this downgrading of their positions, and several left the department for jobs in other agencies.

The reorganization also sought to even out the acreage among the state forests, resulting in the formation of seven new forests in 1965: four in Region I (Bay de Noc, located at Escanaba; Ford River, at Felch; Copper Range [later changed to Mishwabic], at Twin Lakes; and Tahquamenon River, at Newberry) and three in Region II (Betsie River, at Beulah; Jordan River, at Boyne City; and Tittabawassee River, at Gladwin. Another new forest, Region II's Kalkaska State Forest, was added three years later.[22]

The foresters' salaries and civil service classification was not the only controversial issue attending the reorganization. Local citizens expressed their complaints to the commission regarding the shifting of the district offices, particularly those in Baldwin and Traverse City.[23] For many years thereafter, influential conservationists from the Traverse City area vowed to bring about a return of the district office to Traverse City, but such efforts never succeeded.

THE HIGGINS LAKE NURSERY WAS CLOSED IN 1965, LEAVING THE WYMAN Nursery in Manistique and the Southern Michigan Nursery near Brighton to carry on. The decision to close the Higgins Lake Nursery was difficult, given the fact that it had a reputation for producing high-quality red pine planting stock. But there was also a need for jack pine seedlings, and production of jack pine at Higgins Lake had been complicated by the increasing amount of oak in the surrounding forest. (Oaks serve as the alternate host for a rust disease that infects jack pine; no practical way could be seen to prevent the infection of jack pine seedlings at the Higgins Lake Nursery by the oak gall rust.) There was little or no oak in the vicinity of Wyman Nursery, so the Higgins Lake Nursery was closed.[24]

Even with the reduced production, the state nurseries developed a surplus, which soil conservation districts requested permission to purchase for distribution to members. The Michigan Seedling Growers protested, but the Conservation Commission approved the new policy, finding that it was needed for wildlife habitat improvement and that commercial nurseries lacked an adequate supply of plants. The commission also reasoned that landowners were not willing to pay the higher costs presumed to prevail at the private nurseries and that commercial growers did not have a central ordering system.[25] Thus, a disagreement developed between the state and private nursery operators regarding the role of the public nurseries.

IN SPITE OF THE PROBLEMS RELATED TO THE REORGANIZATION, NEW INITIATIVES appeared and progress was made toward bringing the now well-developed state forest resources under scientific management. A special appropriation of fifty thousand dollars was made during the 1965–66 biennium to begin a forest-cover-type mapping project using the new 1964 aerial photos, a management tool that foresters had used for years. Four foresters were hired to do photo interpretation and mapping in several districts. Maps were drafted one square-mile section at a time at a scale of four inches to the mile and then sent to Lansing to be assembled into large township maps by the Engineering Division.[26]

The map project proceeded slowly. One major problem for cartographers was that the lines on the various individual section maps did not match when laid next to the maps for the adjacent sections as a consequence of slight changes of scale from one photo to another. The engineers hated the idea of putting out a shoddy product in which roads and streams did not meet across section lines, while foresters in the field were anxious for even rough maps, which they believed would be very useful. They already knew where the roads were: they wanted the forest cover information. The engineers eventually agreed to send out the imperfect maps, and the state forests had a new tool to use in their continuing quest for better management. These maps enabled foresters to set some general priorities regarding areas to be inspected for potential harvest, forest health concerns, reforestation needs, and recreational opportunities. Timber markets were strong, and there was considerable pressure from people who wished to purchase timber.

In 1962, the Reforestation Fund was renamed the Forest Management Fund and thereafter was available for funding other silvicultural practices in addition to tree planting. Plantations were pruned and released from overhead competition, and hardwood stands were thinned.[27] In fiscal 1968, the appropriation for the Forest Management Fund was $1.25 million.[28] That figure represented the maximum the Forestry Division could legally spend, but the actual amount would depend on the amount of revenue received from the sale of timber on tax-reverted lands. This arrangement created a potential conflict of interest—the state could increase timber sales to make more money—but foresters in the field continued to base their management decisions on the condition and needs of the resource rather than on a need for revenue. During this period, Lansing never put out a plea to the field to raise more money by selling more timber.

In the 1960s, loggers, or timber jobbers, as they were often called, "discovered" most mature and merchantable timber. A jobber would come into the forester's office and say that he had found a really nice patch of aspen, for example, and request a permit to cut it. If the forester was not already familiar with the stand in question, he would check it and approve or disapprove the request based on an assessment of the age and condition of the timber. This procedure was perhaps equivalent to hunting and gathering as a method of management, but it worked, even though the state forest policy said that if two or more people were thought to be interested in a tract, it should be sold at auction. Generally, only one person could be expected to be interested.

Jobbers sometimes thought that building a road into a certain area would enable them to establish a claim to state timber accessible from that road. They thus established individual territories, and others generally did not violate such claims. However, as timber markets improved, more people were attracted to the industry, and conflicts became inevitable. Larger, advertised auction sales generally replaced the small, negotiated sales.

Most timber sales during the 1960s required the foresters and/or technicians to scale the harvested products in the woods before shipment to the mills. This was a time-consuming job for the state forest staff and offered opportunity for theft. A logger could haul a load of logs to a sawmill and say the wood came from his own land—that is, if anyone bothered to ask. If he got it to the mill without being detected, he could avoid paying the stumpage. Not all jobbers engaged in this shady practice, of course, but it happened enough to make the foresters wary.

One way to ensure payment of stumpage was to have a third-party agreement with a timber broker. Brokers had contracts with major mills to supply wood and then subcontracted with timber jobbers to fill those contracts. For their services, the brokers would receive a small amount from the jobber's check. They would also withhold the stumpage and submit it to the area forester. Brokers often made advance payments to jobbers to tide them over tough times. Similar withholding agreements existed directly with mills.

AS APPLIED ON THE STATE FORESTS DURING THE 1950S AND 1960S, SILVIculture was designed to help the recovery of the forest cover. Timber harvests generally removed only a few trees to make growing space available

∾ CONTINUOUS FOREST INVENTORY

Ed Eckart had worked a season or two on the CFI and was considered a seasoned veteran. Harold Kollmeyer, who supervised the CFI operation, had chosen Eckart to introduce yet another bit of technology to this project—beyond the Univac computer at Michigan Tech. By equipping a veteran with a tape recorder with which to record his observations, Kollmeyer could save half his labor cost by sending just one person to remeasure certain plots. Of course, he would save the most on plots where the crew had been least productive—those requiring the best part of a day just to get there. With this new method, only one person would have to spend the time walking in.

Eckart got the nod to pioneer the new technology in 1960. As he recalled,

So, here I am, loaded down not only with all the equipment that two of us used to carry, but also with a fifteen-pound Wollensack tape recorder in a wooden box slung over my shoulder as well. Oh, yeah, there was the second bag that held the battery and the microphone, too. Other stuff I had was the usual tool bag with compass, tally whacker, diameter tape, plot tape, increment borer, two cans of paint, tatum board, maps and aerial photo, my lunch, a bag of IBM punch cards, and five pieces of half-inch pipe to use as plot stakes.

I took all this stuff and worked my way into one of the nastiest tag alder swamps I've ever seen. The old paint marks were very faint and hard to find, but I was able to find my way the couple of miles to the string of five plots, only one of which had any trees at all. The swamp had opened up to an open bog and, as I made my way across to the little desert island with the six trees on it, I broke through the floating mat into the bottomless loon goo. This was where the Wollensack came in handy, as it stopped my descent through the sphagnum mat. It came up against my armpit and acted as a fifteen-pound water wing, arresting my fall, but bruising my arm in the process.

After kicking my way out of the hole I'd made, I half walked, half crawled the fifty yards or so to the little island. Fortunately there was enough dry ground for me to sit

for the rest. Foresters generally marked hardwoods for removal but handled other forest cover types differently. Mixed hardwoods and conifers were often sold on a "three-stick limit," meaning that the jobber could cut any tree that contained three eight-foot pulp sticks to a four-inch diameter top. This strategy provided growing space for smaller (but not necessarily younger) trees throughout the stand. On rare occasions when trees of two

Forester Harold Kollmeyer measuring tree diameter on a permanent one-fifth-acre Continuous Forest Inventory plot on the Lake Superior State Forest, Luce County, Michigan, July 1961. Courtesy of the Michigan Department of Natural Resources.

down in relative comfort, which I did. I then took out the microphone, plugged it into the Wollensack and proceeded to record what I had seen and done—in graphic detail. Next, with one great arm motion, I planted all five of the plot stakes in the bog. Then I wolfed down my lunch and slogged back out of there.

And I think that was the last time we used the Wollensack.

Source: Reprinted by permission from *Michigan Forests* 15, no. 1 (winter 1994).

different ages occurred in a given stand and removing the older ones was desirable, foresters specified diameter limits.

Swamp conifers and jack pine were cut in strips, leaving uncut strips to provide seed and partial shade. Only aspen stands were clear-cut—that is, all trees cut over the stand area. Aspens mature at forty to fifty years of age, and many thousands of acres of aspen were simultaneously approaching maturity. Harvest of aspen was begun fairly aggressively to avoid having large numbers of trees become overmature and fall down. Aspens responded to the harvest by sending up tens of thousands of sprouts, or suckers, per acre. Hand crews were hired to clean up stands after aspen clear-cuts. These crews walked across the harvest sites on snowshoes and cut the small, unmerchantable, residual hardwoods that would shade out the developing aspen stand. In all cases, care was taken to avoid giving the public the impression that the forests were being ravaged. Rather, they were being managed and nurtured.

The Continuous Forest Inventory showed an increase of 2.8 million cords over the first period measured, while 930,000 cords were harvested in the same period.[29] Timber volume obviously was accumulating rapidly. In 1966, state forest timber revenue hit a million dollars for the first time, indicating the markets' strength.[30] As the markets improved and the timber matured, it became clear that foresters would have to get control of the decisions on what stands were to be harvested rather than just responding to requests. Foresters wanted to take the lead, and doing so would require some form of management plan. Continuous Forestry Inventory data showed a growing resource, and the type maps gave a good idea of where it was. All that was needed was a system to put the data together in a meaningful way.

Two different systems evolved during the 1960s. At the west end of the Upper Peninsula, a system known as "block plans" appeared. In this approach, forest managers chose a geographic block of land of between ten and fifty thousand acres and examined every stand in it. These blocks generally shared some common characteristic, such as an upland area in the upper part of a given watershed, or a large swamp downstream, or an area of jack pine plains. The square-mile sections were used as the basic record-keeping unit, and stands were numbered within each section. After the entire block had been examined, treatment priorities could be assigned, and the basis of a plan could be formed.

John Gaffney began this block plan design on the Mishwabic State Forest, and LeRoy Stevens began it on the Baraga State Forest. In 1968 the Mackinac and Tahquamenon River Forests adopted it. Its major advantage was that it organized the foresters' work in the geographic areas they had determined to be most important—first by choosing the block to be examined, and second by ranking treatment needs within that block. The major drawback to the system was that after two or three blocks had been examined, so much work had been identified that it left little time for continuing the block examination.

At the same time, foresters in Region II, under the leadership of Fred H. Haskin, district forester at Cadillac and soon the state's silviculturist in Lansing, were exploring a different system. This "diagnostic inventory" called for the establishment of "compartments" of approximately one thousand acres each, the main record-keeping unit. Ten percent of the compartments, spread randomly across the entire state forest, were to be examined each year. The advantage of this system was its practicality in recognizing the impossibility of visiting the entire area in a short time and spreading the stand examination over a wide area. It also provided a complete examination and plan after ten years and assured distribution of activity and treatment over the entire forest ownership during the intervening years. The disadvantage was that no portion of the forest larger than a compartment ever had an overall up-to-date plan.

The two systems developed simultaneously, with both using the data-gathering forms and procedures outlined by Haskin for the diagnostic inventory. The department reported twelve block plans completed in the Upper Peninsula in 1970.[31] Plans to enter diagnostic inventory data into a computer were gathering support both in the field and in Lansing. A good deal of discussion and even a modest amount of argument took place between the supporters of the two plans, which had taken on regional identities. Finally, recognizing the need to choose one system and apply it statewide, Daw, the state forester, ordered that a decision be made—two separate systems for management planning would be unacceptable. A meeting of the division leaders was held at Cadillac and the randomly distributed compartment system won out. Upper Peninsula foresters were disappointed but acquiesced gracefully.

Under Haskin's leadership, the diagnostic inventory with distributed compartments became the official system in 1971.[32] A long list of codes was established for tree species, tree age, cover types, stand conditions, needed treatments (such as planting or thinning), counties, soil types, topography, and many other factors, enabling the data to be entered into a computer for analysis. An agreement with Michigan Technological University allowed for use of the university's computer and provided technical support. Gerald A. Rose moved from the Michigamme State Forest to Lansing to look after the technical details. Thus, with a few refinements, the operations inventory was born out of the old diagnostic inventory, and organized management replaced the days of hunting and gathering.

Management plans covered more than just timber. Sites with potential for recreational development and natural areas were identified as well. Scenic drives were established in the 1960s, with interpretive signs to explain the management practices visible along the road. One of the more popular drives was in Mackinac County at Big Knob. It was completed in 1966.[33] The shore-to-shore riding/hiking trail was completed in the northern Lower Peninsula and was heavily used by horseback enthusiasts, who conducted annual rides from Lake Huron to Lake Michigan. Forest brochures containing maps and general descriptions of scenic attractions were produced for many of the state forests.

FOUR STATE FORESTS HAD DESIGNATED NATURAL AREAS: THE 135-ACRE Besser Natural Area and 696-acre Bois Lake Nature Study Area in the Black Lake State Forest; the very large (14,137-acre) Betsy Lake Natural Area Preserve in the Lake Superior State Forest; the 160-acre Roscommon Red Pine Natural Area Preserve in the Houghton Lake State Forest; and three areas in the Betsie River State Forest, all on South Manitou Island (Gull Point Nature Study Area, 453 acres; Nature Reservation, 551 acres; and Natural Area Preserve, 1,038 acres).[34]

The 1960s had been a decade of investment in public relations and recreational facilities—stressing the concept that there was more to the state forests than timber. The '70s saw those investments reach maturity. In 1970 the Natural Resources Commission adopted a new policy for managing the state forest lands, which said, in part: "Forests are more than just trees. They include all of the interrelated resources: other plants, soil, water, air, minerals, gas, oil, fish and wildlife. To assure proper management of the state forests for the public good, it is the declared policy of the Michigan Department of Natural Resources to manage the state forests to yield that combination of products and services which best meets the recreational, spiritual, and physical needs of the people now and in the future."[35]

Everyone seemed to be suddenly lined up to get a piece of the state forests for his/her own special interest. Snowmobiles, trail bikes, horsemen, and canoeists were eager to see trails and facilities developed for their use. Oil and gas interests were making application for leases and drilling permits. Hunters pushed for more deer habitat improvement. And, of course, timber companies also wanted attention in the form of advertised timber sales. All of these demands fell on the staff of the Forestry Division.

The first appropriations from the $100 million Recreation Bond Issue of 1968 became available in 1971 through Act 41, P.A. 1970, and it appeared that finally there would be enough money to do things right.[36] Six new campgrounds were built in the 1971–72 biennium, bringing the total to 151 state forest campgrounds.[37] It soon became evident that some controls would be needed on the use of these campgrounds.

One result of this emphasis on recreation was the hiring of two landscape architects to serve on the Forest Management Division staff. Dean Sandell and Dennis Vitton were the first additions to the professional staff in Lansing who did not hold degrees in forestry. Some observers saw this as an erosion of the role and importance of foresters, but most staffers saw the two newcomers as a welcome addition with important knowledge and skills not otherwise available from within the Forestry Division.

On Memorial Day weekend, 1972, an incident occurred in the Houghton Lake State Forest Campground that changed the nature of the state forest campgrounds and their administration. The Natural Resources Commission in their June report relayed that "Dominating the scene was a gang of youth 'toughs' whose intimidation of other campers and generally disorderly conduct forced the DNR to close the campground."[38] The campground had been overcrowded—an estimated 600–800 campers on the 8-acre site—and there were no designated campsites. The campground reopened on June 16th, with a charge of $1.50 per night, direct supervision by an on-duty ranger who was to turn away excess campers, and stepped-up patrols by conservation officers.[39] Similar incidents occurred across the state, resulting in the institution of fees at three other campgrounds as well—Reedsburg Dam, Arbutus #4, and Big Bear Lake.[40] By the end of the decade there were over 170 campgrounds in the system and things were running smoothly.[41]

As the popularity of snowmobiling grew, foresters and others became concerned that, if unregulated, snowmobilers might destroy areas of forest

◌ FACE-OFF AT THE CAMPGROUND

The state forests had a close relationship with the Boy Scouts in many areas, often sharing leadership. The foresters always had a list of projects for which there was no funding, and the scouts always had a need for conservation projects to fulfill requirements for rank advancement or merit badges.

One summer night in the early 1970s, Bill Mahalak, area forester at the Mackinac State Forest, forest technician Harley St. Ours, logger Einar Strom, and schoolteacher/scout leader Bob Nelson were camping with the scouts at Little Brevort Lake. They were just about to turn in for the night when some noisy motorcyclists came into the campground.

Not wanting to see an ugly incident develop or to lose a night's sleep, Mahalak decided that quick action would quiet down the interlopers. He pulled on his pants and boots and instructed Nelson to get in the pickup and drive up to the group with his lights off. Mahalak would walk just ahead. When he gave him the sign, Nelson would turn on the lights, and Mahalak would swing into action.

When the lights came on, they revealed about a dozen choppers and as many heavily tattooed bikers armed with chains and spears. They were temporarily blinded by the headlights, but Mahalak thought, "Holy sockeye, I'm in big trouble now!" What he did, however, was roar, "There's people in this campground trying to sleep, so you'll have to quiet down or leave!" hoping no one would see or hear his knees shaking. "OK, Sir, some of us are staying and the others will be leaving," came the response.

"Wow," Mahalak thought. "I'm pretty impressive after all, I guess!" Then he glanced behind him and saw that St. Ours and Strom were standing behind him with feet spread apart and axes in their hands. There was no further trouble, and the bikers who stayed overnight left quietly in the morning.

regeneration and shatter the tranquility of winter in the northwoods. There were incidents of apparent vandalism—or extreme stupidity—in which snowmobiles were driven along rows of young trees, breaking them down, but they were relatively few. In fact, the snow machines tended to limit themselves by their inability to travel through deep fluffy snow. This was especially true of the high horsepower models.

Capitalizing on these weaknesses—the inherent difficulty of traveling through deep snow and the desire of the riders for high-powered machines, the DNR established a system of groomed trails. This provided good riding conditions for enthusiasts while controlling the areas in which they were used.

DNR field people were frustrated by the snowmobiles' tendency to bury themselves, but purchasing agents found it difficult to understand why machines with small engines were to be preferred over more powerful models. They delivered the bigger machines more than once to unappreciative foresters, technicians, and biologists.

Trail bikes posed a more serious control problem than snowmobiles, since they are able to travel nearly anywhere on dry ground. Controlling these vehicles required more thought. In December 1972, a set of rules in draft form was presented to the Natural Resources Commission. In general, the proposed rules restricted vehicles to areas posted as open to their use and required them, when parked, to be within fifty feet of an area posted as open. Snowmobiles were restricted to areas with at least four inches of snow.

The Sierra Club supported the proposed rules, but motorcycle groups considered them to be discriminatory and not in the best interest of natural resources. The Great Lakes Motorcycle Association was one group that criticized the proposal but also offered to work with the DNR to come up with a better solution.[42]

In April 1973 the Commission approved rules governing the use of off-road vehicles on state forest land that would "require operators of wheeled off-road vehicles (ORVs) to yield the right-of-way to environmental values and steer clear of a collision course with other outdoor recreationists in Michigan's northern State forests." The new rules allowed ORVs on any roads not posted as closed, and it prohibited stream crossings except over bridges or culverts. It also required permits from the Department of Natural Resources for organized events.[43]

Some ORV enthusiasts considered the rules to be too restrictive—particularly where stream crossings were concerned. They reasoned that in the absence of a bridge or culvert, they could *walk* a motorcycle across a stream without causing any damage. Thus the Commission was persuaded to change Rule 10(b) to read "To enter or to cross any stream except over a bridge, culvert or similar structure, or by walking the vehicle across without power applied to the drive wheel or wheels, or as may be authorized by the director." Owners of four-wheel vehicles asked at a public hearing in July 1973 how they should "walk" a jeep across a stream.[44]

And so the issue simmered, with confusion on all sides as to where a person could and could not ride a trail bike. Was it only permitted on roads posted as open, or was everything open unless posted closed? Could they cross a stream or not? Was it the same in the Upper Peninsula as in the Lower Peninsula? Nearly 1,300 people attended public hearings in Marquette, Gaylord, and Lansing regarding rules for trail bikes. Most spoke in opposition. An advisory group was formed. Letters poured in.[45]

Some foresters wryly observed that the best thing that could happen to a special interest group was that their activity would demonstrate a potential for environmental damage and thus require licensing and regulation. Once they had a licensing act, they could vote themselves an increase in license fees to be earmarked for facility development. Thus they could pressure the DNR to provide services for activities that the department might not favor on state lands. In fact, the Great Lakes Four-Wheel Drive Association said in a presentation to the Commission in October 1974 that they would like to have legislation requiring registration.[46]

Robert M. Tyler, a forester and a trail bike enthusiast himself, was moved to Lansing to lead the development of trails and facilities for ORVs.

Similar struggles were taking place on Michigan's rivers between canoeists and fishermen. Special plans were drawn up for the Au Sable River, where extensive frontage was acquired from Consumers Power Company in exchange for rights-of-way across state lands in the northern Lower Peninsula.[47] Deputy Director Warren Shapton criticized the campgrounds along the Au Sable saying, "camping must either be limited or transferred back from the stream."[48] Redesign of campgrounds along the Au Sable and Manistee Rivers continued over the next few years, with many canoe camps being either relocated away from the rivers or rebuilt with designated sites. Five new river campgrounds were also constructed.[49]

In 1972 the Jordan River was dedicated as a wild-scenic river under the provisions of the Natural Rivers Act of 1970 and similar designation for the Betsie River was tentatively approved in 1973.[50] The Two-Hearted River was designated a "Wilderness River" in 1974 followed by a similar proposal for the Fox in 1975.[51] These natural river designations generally meant more work for the forest administrators. For example, the Jordan River rules stated, "The Area Forester of the Jordan River State Forest is recommended to serve as Zoning Administrator."[52]

An area of about 2,775 acres in Grand Traverse and Kalkaska Counties was given special status as a "Quiet Area" in 1973. The newly designated "Sand Lakes Quiet Area" would allow timber management on small areas, but no new roads were to be built and ORV trails would not be constructed.[53]

The state forests were assuming a major role in Michigan's outdoor recreation.

INTEREST IN OIL AND GAS LEASING INCREASED SHARPLY IN THE NORTHERN part of Region II while all the confusion over recreational uses was going on. Geological formations dictated that leasing units would be eighty acres. That meant there could be as many as eight wells per square mile. Wildlife officials and interested citizens expressed concern to the Commission.[54]

The Natural Resources Commission adopted a resolution in October 1970 ordering the State Supervisor of Wells to suspend issuance of drilling permits on state lands in the elk range (north of townline 30 in Alpena and Montmorency Counties and north of townline 29 in Antrim and Otsego Counties) and ordered the DNR to do a "sweeping study" of the effects of oil and gas development on wildlife populations. They also ordered DNR to find out whether it would be legal to suspend drilling permits on lands already leased for such activity.[55]

The following June, the Commission approved a policy allowing permits to be denied, but on an individual basis; not with a blanket policy.[56] More controversy; more confusion. And the state forests were in the middle of it all. Area foresters were responsible to inspect every potential well site and estimate the volume and value of timber to be removed. Sometimes they would recommend a different site; sometimes denial of a permit would be recommended.

Many of the oil company representatives came from other parts of the country, where forest values were not a consideration. They did not understand the foresters' jargon; the foresters did not understand theirs, making it difficult to communicate. In 1971 the Forestry Division established a position in the regional office at Roscommon to assist the communications between DNR and the oil companies and also between DNR and the recreation interests. Michael D. Moore was the forester assigned to this position.

In the summer of 1972 a proposal was brought before the Commission to make a special dedication of 129 square miles of state forest land in Cheboygan, Otsego, and Montmorency Counties as a quiet area with little or no noise from oil and gas development. Ford Kellum, a retired game biologist from the DNR now representing the Michigan Audubon Society, and Dave Smethurst, chairman of the Pigeon River Association, were prominent advocates for this special designation.[57] This proposal stirred quite a controversy and led to heated exchange between the oil men and the DNR. At issue was whether it was legal for the state to deny drilling permits after having leased drilling rights years before.

In response to the proposal and in hopes of stemming the controversy, Ray E. Pfeifer, of the Forestry Division's Lansing staff, presented a proposed plan for the Pigeon River area to the Commission in May 1973. Pfeifer explained that the Pigeon River area was unique in two ways: it was home to the largest elk herd east of the Mississippi, and it was a large block of land in the northern Lower Peninsula with 90 percent state ownership.

The objectives of the plan were to maintain the elk herd and provide protection for other wildlife, protect and maintain the natural beauty of the area, and develop the best combination of uses. Other provisions of the plan included an attempt to include the area's three streams under the provisions of the Natural Rivers Act, creation of a local advisory committee, maintenance of existing campgrounds, reduction of vehicle access, and an attempt to designate "wild areas" with the area. Pfeifer received good cooperation from the oil companies in development of this plan.[58]

Six months later, in December 1973, the Pigeon River Country State Forest was formed from portions of the old Pigeon River, Hardwood, Black Lake, and Thunder Bay River state forests. The old Pigeon River forest was renamed the Otsego State Forest.[59] Headquarters for the new state forest were established at the old Pigeon River headquarters, a group of three log buildings constructed by the Civilian Conservation Corps on the bank of the Pigeon River in the heart of the forest. Ned Caveney was appointed the Area Forester and soon moved into the residence at the headquarters.

Gradually, the foresters and geologists worked out procedures that softened the effects of oil and gas development across the northern Lower Peninsula. Tanks and other facilities were painted in colors that blended with the natural surroundings, mufflers were installed on pumps, and access roads were constructed with slight curves to screen well sites from the main roads. The development of oil and gas resources under the state forests became just one more activity of the forest managers.

ADDING TO THE ALREADY FULL SCHEDULE OF THE STATE FOREST MAN-agers was a new initiative adopted early in 1971 by the Wildlife Division of the DNR that proposed to double the deer herd. "A million deer by 1980" was the slogan that implied a need for improving deer habitat through increased timber harvest and shorter timber rotations.[60]

Under the state forest management policy passed by the Commission in 1970, the Wildlife Division had an equal voice with Forestry in management decisions on state forest land.[61] Biologists used that voice to push for management for aspen in nearly every place where it was possible. Aspen, which forms excellent deer habitat, was often found mixed with maple, oak, white pine, and other species. Foresters had two management options in such cases—remove just the aspens to provide growing space for the longer-lived and more economically valuable maple and oak, or clearcut the stands to favor the sun-loving aspens, which would send up sprouts from the roots to occupy the entire area harvested. One healthy aspen tree, when cut, could send up enough sprouts to cover an area with a radius equivalent to the height of the tree.

Generally, foresters agreed with the biologists on the decisions to manage for aspens, but there were differences of opinion when aspen was a minor component of the forest stand and other components were high-value species. Heated arguments occurred at times, each side considering the other to be single-minded and uncooperative. Foresters criticized biologists for failing to consider values other than game species, and biologists returned the argument saying foresters were interested only in selling timber. Foresters noted that, while managing for wildlife and game was a part of their job as managers of the forest, consideration of commercial values was not a part of the Wildlife Division's responsibility. Therefore, the outcome of the arguments was more often than not in favor of Wildlife.

Adding to the difficulty over aspen management was the biologists' insistence on "cleaning up" the stands after clearcutting. Foresters readily acknowledged that residual hardwoods too small to harvest posed a threat to developing aspen stands because of the tendency of their crowns to spread, shading out the young aspens. In fact, removal of such residual hardwoods was a normal part of the silviculture practiced on the state forests.[62] Conifers, however, were a different story.

Foresters felt it desirable to leave occasional balsam fir or white pine trees in aspen clearcuts for aesthetic purposes. These trees had a lower propensity to spread their crowns and occupy large areas, they argued, and their presence lent some diversity to the areas. Biologists considered them to be potential death traps for grouse—perches where hawks could sit undetected and swoop down on grouse chicks. Wildlife Division paid to have many hundreds of acres bulldozed to kill young white pine and balsam fir in aspen harvest areas, occasionally causing local controversy because of the unattractive appearance or loss of favorite trees from the landscape.

A large research project was begun as a part of the deer habitat program in the 1973–74 biennium. This project was conceived to study the effects of clearcutting on the deer herd and on public opinion. Paired treatments one-quarter township (9 square miles) in size were to be treated with 75 percent, 50 percent, and 25 percent of the uplands clearcut while another pair of quarter-townships, where normal timber management activity took place, would serve as the control, or comparison, treatments.[63] Quarter-township treatment areas needed to be nearly solid state ownership and in areas considered to be high deer potential.

Foresters in whose areas the study tracts fell were ordered to set up and administer the cutting of these unusually large blocks of land—blocks which would not have been treated in this way under normal state forest management practices. Most of the treatment areas were sold commercially, but where stands of timber could not be sold, they were bulldozed.

Many foresters felt betrayed by their leaders in Lansing for having allowed this to happen, but it was approved by the DNR's front office and therefore was an official Department program and as such was supported by Forestry Division. As was the case with other wildlife management activities that aimed at keeping forest cover off the land, foresters felt this program mocked their efforts at forest restoration. One forester observed that most research is done on a scale smaller than normal operations. This project did the opposite—researching practices that would never be implemented even if proven effective.

Area Forester Don Torchia, on the Houghton Lake State Forest, handled the bulk of the operations on the wildlife research project. "This was my first assignment upon being promoted to the Area Forester position. My role was to see that the harvest of 5 of the cutting units was completed by January of 1975. Markets were poor for small oak, resulting in thousands of cords being cut and left on the ground. I coordinated the cutting operations among the various timber jobbers involved. I helped them with markets and at times used state equipment to maintain roads being used to haul timber out in order to settle conflicts. I met the deadline, but was delayed in starting the Operations Inventory on the Houghton Lake Forest because of this project."[64]

In 1976 the Wildlife Division reported the following: "The intensive deer habitat management research study started last biennium continues. All of the forest treatment is completed on the six paired quarter-townships. They have been clearcut at 25, 50, and 75 percent rates of intensity. Deer numbers have increased considerably and at a faster rate on these research units compared to the rest of northern Michigan. The success of hunters in both bagging and seeing deer on the research units has increased each year since the study began. Vegetation surveys continue. Three studies investigated the behavior and attitude responses of firearm deer hunters, other forest recreationists, and property owners to the experimental clearcutting."[65]

Torchia never saw a final report on the quarter-township cutting project, but heard this from a hunter using one of the large clearcuts: "The habitat is great and we're seeing lots of deer, but if we should shoot one, I don't know where we'd find a tree to hang it up!"

IN THE SPRING OF 1974 THE FORESTRY DIVISION MADE AN EXPERIMENTAL planting of hybrid aspens developed by the Institute of Paper Chemistry in Appleton, Wisconsin. The planting was done on two sites in the Betsie River State Forest in Manistee County. The rationale for this trial was that fast-growing hybrids might be used to fill in gaps in aspen resource availability which could be seen on the horizon. Several such plantings were made over the next decade in various parts of the state, and, while there were some successes, the program never was implemented on an operational scale.

Adding to the foresters' woes was the use of state forest land as a burial site for livestock contaminated with the fire retardant polybrominated

Foresters gather for their annual meeting at the Conservation School at Higgins Lake, 1966. These training sessions, generally held at the end of winter, provided a forum for consistency of operations. Courtesy of the Michigan Department of Natural Resources.

biphenyl (PBB) in 1974. PBB had accidentally been mixed with cattle feed in place of a feed supplement. Thousands of head of cattle were slaughtered and buried in clay-lined pits on state forest land near the communities of Kalkaska and Mio. The burials required a considerable amount of the foresters' time in administration and was viewed by most as one more in a series of insults on the recovering forest resource. Off-road vehicles, oil and gas wells, quarter-township clearcuts, and now disposal of contaminated cattle—it seemed as if the forests had become a collection place for undesirable activities. Everything seemed to be controversial. Even their forest restoration activities were looked on by some as undesirable.

Biologists despised the practice of planting red pine in old openings, referring to planted pines as "biological deserts" because of the lack of undergrowth habitat in such stands. Their concern was intensified with adoption of the million deer by 1980 goal, but there were still concerns about prairie chickens and sharptail grouse as well. The Game Division reported in 1970 that the sharptails were "not doing well," having suffered a 10 percent drop in population in 1969 and another 10 percent loss in 1970.[66] A special management area was proposed for prairie chickens in Missaukee County in

December, 1976.[67] Despite the best efforts of biologists to save a remnant population, the prairie chickens were still listed as declining in 1980.[68]

Foresters gathered every year at the Conservation Training School at Higgins Lake, generally during the last week of March, to coincide with "spring breakup" time, when many roads were impassable and little activity could take place in the woods. Presentations were designed to increase the participants' technical knowledge and challenge them intellectually. A strong camaraderie developed among the foresters at these meetings, and much information was traded on market conditions, characteristics of certain timber jobbers, new technology, and innovative ideas. The meetings also provided opportunities for socializing, and many strong friendships grew out of such gatherings.

The endangered species acts passed by the federal government in 1973 and the state in 1974 brought attention to the tiny Kirtland's warbler, known to nest only on the jack pine plains of the northeastern Lower Peninsula. The state adopted a goal of 1,000 breeding pairs to be considered as a safe population level that would trigger removal from the endangered list. Jack pines, although only forming suitable habitat for perhaps five to ten years in their early development, were to be managed to an age of 50 years and approximately 135,000 acres of state land would be managed for them.[69]

Early in the Department's management for "the warbler," controversy arose over whether jack pine stands in the warbler habitat areas could be harvested before being treated with fire or planted with jack pine seed or seedlings. Biologists at first insisted on burning standing trees in order to copy the natural system as closely as possible. It soon became apparent, however, that it was impractical to treat all the necessary acres in that fashion and a very practical system of commercial harvest followed by planting was developed. The planting pattern was termed the "opposing wave," creating openings at approximately sixty-foot spacing. Since warblers were known to nest on the edge of a small opening, this pattern proved to be very attractive and productive.

Jack pine management underwent close scrutiny in the early '70s. Prior to the development of interest in managing sites for the Kirtland's warbler, foresters in the Upper Peninsula began working on effective and efficient ways to regenerate the maturing jack pine resource after harvest. The Lake Superior forest, in particular, took this issue on and eventually solved it.

∾ THE GREAT SKIT CONTEST

Disagreements over red pine notwithstanding, foresters and biologists were, for the most part, good friends. Biologists often showed up at the Forestry Division's annual meetings, and foresters sometimes attended meetings of the Wildlife Division. These visits generally took place after normal working hours, when refreshments and visiting time were available. On one such occasion, whose date and place have been lost to the ages, a discussion of which division possessed the greater talent led to a challenge to see which division could perform the better skit for the other. The key parties involved were Merrill L. Petoskey, chief of the Wildlife Division, and Robert A. Borak, regional forester for Forestry Division's Region II at Roscommon.

Wildlife went first, presenting a drama one evening at the Forestry Division annual meeting at Higgins Lake in March 1974. Several months earlier, after a staff meeting somewhere in Region II, there had been a notable arm-wrestling bout between Borak and habitat biologist Bob Odom from Traverse City. Odom had won both right-handed and left-handed.

As the skit began the scene was explained: Department of Natural Resources Deputy Director Chuck Harris, dressed in a black and white striped referee shirt, explained that he had grown very weary of the constant bickering between the two divisions over the planting of red pine. He proposed an arm-wrestling match to settle the matter. He then asked for a volunteer from Forestry to meet Wildlife's representative. Before anyone could respond, Harris grabbed Borak's arm and pulled him to the front of the room. Everyone cheered.

Harris asked who would represent Wildlife. After an awkward silence there was a commotion at the back of the room followed by the appearance of a six-foot gorilla (actually Odom in costume). The big ape lumbered toward the front of the room, glowering to the right and left but especially straight ahead, where Borak had jumped up to the top of a table and was wildly swinging a banjo left there from an earlier skit and frantically calling for help from his supervisor, Troy Yoder, the regional manager, who was nowhere in sight.

District Forester Raymond Norkoli started a system of alternate strips about 100 feet wide. Strips were clearcut, leaving uncut strips of the same width. The idea was that the uncut strips would provide seed to regenerate the cut strips; when the regeneration in the cut strips was old enough to bear seed,

Harris quieted the crowd and explained the rules to the contestants, emphasizing the importance of this event to the future of red pine planting across the entire state. If Borak could not beat the gorilla, there would be no more planting of red pine. Of course, Borak could not and did not beat the gorilla with either hand, but before declaring Wildlife the winner, Harris asked if someone else could better represent Forestry and the interest of red pine.

A hush fell over the room as Robert Leeson, area forester from Baldwin, stood and made his way to the front. Leeson was about sixty years old, stood about five feet six inches tall, and weighed about 130 pounds. Those close to him knew he had a keen sense of humor, most of his colleagues knew him as a pleasant but very quiet person. He wore a deep frown as he weaved his way among the chairs. Was the group about to be scolded for all this frivolity?

Leeson crouched behind the lectern for a few seconds, then leapt to the side with a sudden roar, ripping the buttons from his shirt to reveal a bright blue leotard with the Superman logo. The gorilla gaped in disbelief as Superman pulled a red pine branch from under the lectern and inhaled deeply while holding the pine to his nose. He took several deep breaths of the red pine aroma, roaring more loudly with each successive dose. His chest swelled. Finally, the gorilla fled the scene, unwilling to meet Superman's challenge. Thus, the fate of the red pine was left in the hands of the foresters.

In January 1975, Forestry responded. The scene was a Wildlife staff meeting in 1981. It seemed that the goal of a million deer had been met by 1980, but then the population had collapsed through a series of management errors. Seeking to save face, the staff were working on a plan to hold open season on long-tailed rats, with a goal of a billion long-tailed rats by the year 2000. Players included Borak; Mike Moore, Borak's assistant; Bill Botti, special project forester at Traverse City; Bill Mittig, area forester at Boyne City; and Jerry Divine, assistant area forester at Boyne City.

No winner was declared, but good laughs were had by all. Borak wrote to those who had helped, "I'm sure that at least a few small bonds of goodwill were firmly established."

---

the other strips would be harvested. In this way, the shocking effect of a total clearcut could be avoided and a source of seed would be assured.

The strip cutting appeared to be working at first, but before the young jack pines reached the seed-bearing stage, an outbreak of the jack pine budworm occurred in the strip-cut area. Budworm larvae rained down from the uncut strips and devoured the young jack pines.

Peter C. Grieves and later Robert S. Caouette took over management of the Lake Superior in the late '60s and looked into other methods of regenerating jack pine. They borrowed several ideas from foresters in Ontario. The most successful was a soil scarifier made of ships' anchor chains weighing thirty pounds per link. This was pulled across a clearcut site behind a large log skidder to expose a mineral soil seedbed and break down the pine branches, bringing the jack pine cones in contact with the ground. The sun's rays heated the cones sufficiently to cause them to open and release their seeds, thus starting a new stand of jack pine. This operation served to reduce fire hazard as well.

Local people were shocked at the sight of clearcuts of forty acres and more and they made their concerns known to the DNR. Caouette quickly organized field trips for local residents in order to point out the newly germinated jack pines in the treated areas. Thus reassured that this was not a repeat of the exploitation of the resource that had taken place seventy years before, Newberry residents became solid supporters of the clearcutting and scarification practice. Similar procedures were later adopted in other parts of the state.

A NEW TIMBER SALE PROCEDURE WAS ADOPTED BY THE COMMISSION IN 1974, discontinuing the Commission approval requirement for all sales except those on islands other than Drummond Island. Sales over $1,000 in estimated value would be approved by the Director or his designated representative, which was generally one of the Lansing staff of the Forestry Division.[70]

Forest management activities continued in spite of the controversies over clearcutting, off-road vehicles, oil and gas development, natural rivers, and tree planting. Nine kinds of permits were being issued on state forest land—from timber sales and firewood cutting to gravel removal. It was a dizzying list of demands being placed on the state forests and their managers, signaling a complete turnabout from the days when nobody wanted this land. Now everyone wanted it. Into this maelstrom rode a new leader who would take over as state forester and chief of the Forestry Division.

10

Forest Resource Planning

1975–1990

STATE FORESTER TED DAW RETIRED IN 1975 AFTER MORE THAN FORTY-FIVE
years with the Conservation and Natural Resources Departments. The leaders at the Natural Resources Commission, the Department of Natural Resources (DNR) front office, and the Michigan Legislature believed that the
next state forester should come from outside the agency, thereby introduc-
ing new ideas and a fresh outlook. Both G. S. McIntire and Daw had been
promoted from within, and while many observers felt that the Forestry Division had several good in-house candidates, the position went to Dr. Henry
H. (Hank) Webster, head of the Department of Forestry at Iowa State University. Webster was a forest economist and an academician who spoke a
language not always familiar to or readily understood by the field forces,
but staff spirits nevertheless generally remained high as a new era in state
forest administration began to unfold.

In October 1975, after a few months in office, Webster reported to the Natural Resources Commission on "more effective state forest management." His remarks included the observations that recreation and timber management had shown marked improvement and that forest potential was increasing rapidly. He noted that Michigan's 3.75 million acres of dedicated state forest ranked first in the nation and that Michigan was strong in forestry education with programs in three state universities. However, he also noted some needs, especially in the field of planning. The state forests needed planning for land use, recreation facilities, and environmental protection, most notably in those areas where use exceeded capacity. He suggested four steps for improved effectiveness: (1) better forest resource management planning; (2) more effective utilization of timber growth and regional economic development; (3) more effective recreation planning and environmental protection for state forests; and (4) improved organization.[1]

While emphasizing the need to do better planning for recreational development on the state lands, Webster did not lose sight of the economic potential of Michigan's forestlands, which he felt were being underutilized. In January 1976, he reported to the Natural Resources Commission that he wished to contract with the world's leading forestry consultants, Jaako Pöyry and Company of Helsinki, Finland, to explore solutions to Michigan's forestry problems, particularly in terms of better utilization of poor-quality wood resources. The cost of such a study was estimated at $250,000.[2]

The following month, State Representative Russell L. (Rusty) Hellman of Dollar Bay spoke to the commission in favor of the multiple use of the state forests, saying that the commission was not giving adequate attention to the oil, gravel, mining, and forest resources.[3] Hellman was chair of the House Subcommittee on Natural Resources Appropriations and became a very influential advocate for the state forests. Along with Senator Joe Mack and the powerful chair of the House Appropriations Committee, Dominic Jacobetti, Hellman formed what was sometimes known facetiously as the "Upper Peninsula mafia" in the legislature.

In 1974, Hellman had sponsored a special appropriation of three hundred thousand dollars to start a program he called Forest Cultivation that was intended to make investments in timber management in the state forests. More than eight thousand acres were treated that first year, most of them hardwood stands that were thinned to shorten the time required to produce merchantable products.[4] In most cases, the material cut from these hardwood stands was left on the ground because no market for it existed.

In explaining the rationale behind the Forest Cultivation program, Hellman often told a story of a farmer who received a visit from his pastor. Commenting on the lush stands of corn and wheat, the pastor said, "Isn't it wonderful what you and the Lord have accomplished?" To which the farmer replied, "Yes, and you should've seen it when the Lord had it all to Himself!" In the same way that the farmer needed to take control of his cropland, the state needed to control its forestland, Hellman noted.

At the beginning of the Forest Cultivation program, the Forestry Division arranged with Michigan Technological University (located in Hellman's 110th Legislative District) to monitor the results. The university was contracted to remeasure the old Continuous Forest Inventory plots in Houghton and Baraga Counties and to establish special growth-monitoring plots in the treated areas.[5]

In 1976, with funding for the Forest Cultivation program at $1 million, division officials decided to create forest cultivation teams of foresters who would mark the hardwoods for thinning. William B. Botti transferred to Lansing from Traverse City and assumed leadership of the Forest Cultivation team operation and program. This approach would permit the tracking of funds and assure that none of the money designated for Forest Cultivation was diverted to other activities. The alternative would have been to spread the money into the state forest budgets and assign a certain number of acres to each area. Staff would have been added in appropriate numbers to accomplish the work. The disadvantage of the team approach was the monotony of the work, which eventually led to low productivity. Hellman maintained close contact with the division office to monitor progress, frequently complaining about lack of productivity but steadfastly refusing to endorse any movement away from the team concept. In February 1977, he told Botti that he had decided to cancel the program for the coming year because costs were too high and because jack pine reforestation had been added to the list of activities funded under Forest Cultivation.[6]

Hellman did not follow through on his threat, and the Forest Cultivation program's activities were broadened to include reforestation as well as relatively short-term investments such as thinning of hardwoods and release of red pine plantations from overhead competition, with annual goals set by the program leader in Lansing. The team approach was officially abandoned in 1979 in favor of spreading the funds into the state forest budgets to achieve enhanced coordination.[7]

In June 1977, Dr. Nils Osara reported Jaako Pöyry's findings to the Natural Resources Commission. The study showed a need to use the state's forest resources to diversify the economy. A surplus of small hardwoods needed thinning. New logging techniques were needed, as were competent people to carry them out.[8]

The report described the condition of Michigan's forests as "poor" as a consequence of low quality and small size resulting from the relatively recent exploitation.[9] "In Michigan, the growing of wood is at present commonly considered a nonprofitable venture, so investments in forestry are made on a very limited scale only. But the situation . . . cannot be improved unless considerable investments are made."[10] The report continued, "There are several reasons for the poor forest management. The most important ones are the low demand for small and low quality wood and the low stumpage prices. But there are also other factors, e.g., lack of tradition in this field. Therefore, even the rather limited funds for [timber stand improvement] work are not fully utilized."[11]

The Forest Cultivation program, while started prior to completion of the Jaako Pöyry report, exemplified the type of work needed to lift the state's hardwood forest resources out of the low-quality trap into which the events of the previous three-fourths of a century had plunged them. First had come the commercial clear-cutting of the stands for charcoal production, followed by wildfires and then by intensive cattle grazing. The trees that remained after these insults had been injured by fire and cattle hooves and were thus susceptible to decay. As the trees grew, they became crowded and gradually developed into larger, stunted, poor-quality trees.

State Forester Webster often referred to the "backward-facing funding source" of the state forests, pointing out the relationship between the present forests and the conditions and practices that had prevailed fifty years earlier. Poor forest management practices had spawned poor-quality forests; the only way out of the situation was to invest in upgrading the quality of those forests. Hellman supported Webster's recommendations.[12]

Appearing before the Natural Resources Commission in July 1977, Hellman said, "A decision must be made *now* on whether to give serious consideration of forest restoration and cultivation that would promote forests to the condition that would make it profitable to grow wood of high quality."[13] He requested a letter of intent from the commission that would indicate an intent to follow the recommendations of the Jaako Pöyry study. Dr. Howard Tanner, the DNR director, stated that a letter was being sent to the governor and members of the legislature informing them of the Jaako Pöyry study and stating the department's intention to follow the recommendations therein. The commission supported this action.[14]

The rate of progress did not satisfy Rusty Hellman, a man not known for his patience. In March 1978, he again appeared at a commission meeting, urging implementation of the Jaako Pöyry report. Surely some way could be found to utilize the wood that was being cut in the process of the hardwood thinning being carried out under the Forest Cultivation program. "Three hundred twenty-five thousand tons of cut wood has been left on the ground because it is useless," he scolded. "Forest products cannot grow in Michigan unless something is done to help the resource. A conclusion has not been reached because of the lack of interest."[15]

WEBSTER PICKED UP AND CARRIED ON THE VISION STATED IN 1917 BY former state forester Marcus Schaaf, who had predicted that the planting of pines taking place in 1917 would show a profit around 1977. Time had proved him right. Webster saw the state forests' potential to strengthen and diversify Michigan's economy. He also saw the preponderance of poor-quality hardwood and worked to create markets for it and thereby enhance the forests' productivity. Commenting on the issue of quality, Webster quipped, "If we don't change our direction, we're doomed to arrive where we're headed!" The state forests were headed for a future of poor quality if the DNR did not change direction by removing the low-quality trees.

In April 1978, M. L. "Pete" Petoskey, assistant chief of the Bureau of Resource Management, discussed the use of wood chips as an energy source at a meeting of the Natural Resources Commission. With him were Harry Morey, founder of the Total Chips Company, and Peter Ratcliffe of Morbark Industries, manufacturer of wood chippers and other machinery. Petoskey pointed out how well the harvest of wood for energy chips would fit with the needs of the state forests. State Representative John M. Engler (later Michigan's governor) encouraged the DNR to use this technology.[16]

A thinning trial was established on state forestland in Kalkaska County in June 1977 using the chipping technology. An overcrowded pole-size stand of northern hardwoods was thinned by Total Chips, and the trees removed were hauled away as chips. Both Total Chips and Morbark had hoped that the trial would lead to the DNR's endorsement of the thinning technique. Foresters held off on the endorsement, however, because of extensive root wounds caused by the felling/bunching machine. Nothing could be found in the forestry literature that would indicate the degree of decay that might result from these wounds.

The foresters' reluctance to embrace a process that might be just what they needed to increase growth and quality of their hardwood stands (but also might fill them with heart rot) caused considerable controversy and a flood of angry letters, phone calls, and visits to the commission. The foresters held their ground, stating that thinning provided no advantage if it would lower the quality of the remaining trees. The controversy eventually blew over. Study plots were set up for future measurement, and thinning for chips became common practice on the state forests, with workers taking greater care to avoid damaging the remaining trees.

WEBSTER ALSO GAVE ATTENTION TO THE MANAGEMENT OF THE FOREST resource in the face of low budgets and hiring freezes. In 1977 the department merged the Forestry and Forest Fire Divisions into the Forest Management Division. At the same time, Webster reorganized the state forests, reducing them in number from thirty-one to six, essentially comparable to the former forest districts. The Copper Country State Forest covered the west end of the Upper Peninsula with headquarters in Baraga; the Escanaba River State Forest, with headquarters in Escanaba, included the central Upper Peninsula; and the Lake Superior State Forest, centered at Newberry, covered the east end of the Upper Peninsula. The Mackinaw State Forest, with offices at Gaylord, covered the northern tip of the Lower Peninsula (Region II); the Pere Marquette State Forest, centered at Cadillac, covered the southwestern part of Region II; and the Au Sable State Forest, headquartered at Mio, covered southeastern Region II. Each of the new state forests was staffed with specialists for fire and recreation, planning, silviculture, and private land assistance. Most of the former state forest offices remained open as "forest area" offices named for the town in which they were located.

Many of the staff from the former Forest Fire Division had previously worked to some extent on the state forest recreation program, including road grading and campground construction. Thus, many of the forest fire officers were somewhat familiar with the forest recreation program and blended in well. The merger of Forestry and Forest Fire Divisions eliminated the need for one of the district supervisors in each of the six districts. A program of cross-training enabled forest technicians to work on fire control and fire officers to help with timber management.

About the same time as this reorganization was occurring, Webster introduced a new concept in management planning on the state forests, which he called "key value." The idea behind the key value approach was to separate conflicting uses. It was based on a 1975 book by Marion Clawson, *Forests for Whom and for What?* Clawson was a past director of the Federal Bureau of Land Management and was on the staff of Resources for the Future, a nonprofit research organization based in Washington, D.C.[17] According to Webster, three categories of uses existed—intensive recreation, wilderness, and intensive vegetative management—and each, if pushed to the maximum, would eliminate opportunities for the others. Planners were to use these designations when crafting plans for the state forests.

The key value concept, although basically sound, caused about as much confusion as it solved. Very few parts of the state forests actually were dedicated to the maximum use of any of the three categories, so the vast majority of the land wound up designated "general use," a category that had to be inserted to make the idea work. But how did "general use" differ from the old "multiple use"?

The key value idea might have made a good deal more sense if it had been applied to all state lands rather than just state forests. Those lands deemed best suited for intensive recreation and wilderness had, for the most part, already been transferred to the Parks Division—for example, Interlochen, Muskallonge Lake, Tahquamenon Falls, and North Higgins Lake State Parks. The absence of such lands in the state forest system made it appear that state forest managers had given little attention to these uses and may have contributed to the perceived need to designate tracts as "old-growth" in the next decade. Key value faded completely from view by 1990.

FEMALE FORESTERS AND TECHNICIANS BECAME A REALITY IN THE AGENCY in the late 1970s. The first women were employed on the Forest Inventory and Analysis project, a joint federal-state periodic monitoring of the amount and growth of standing timber, losses resulting from insects and disease, and a variety of other measurements. In October 1978, Patricia Thompson was hired as a forester on the renewable resource inventory crew, and Sybil Abdul-Baki was hired at as a forest technician. Additional hires included Nancy Havlik Garlock, Ruthann French, Ruth Wood, and Linda Tatum. The heretofore all-male workforce had some difficulty accepting these female counterparts, but in a relatively short period of time, the women professionals and technicians earned the respect of their coworkers. Hank Webster was fond of saying that the profession of forestry had "cut itself off from half of the brains in the world" by remaining almost entirely male.

ONE OF THE WORST PERIODS OF AUSTERITY IN THE HISTORY OF THE department struck in late 1980. As a consequence of a huge shortfall in the state's budget caused largely by a decline in the U.S. auto industry, cuts sliced across state government. Many employees were laid off, and others bumped coworkers who had less seniority, often into other divisions or geographic locations. Forest technicians with up to eight years seniority were laid off. Most of the relatively new female employees were laid off. Addressing the Conservation Commission on January 8, 1981, Tanner observed "a catastrophic dynamic change in structure of DNR . . . mostly out of DNR control, that clearly affects the welfare of our public employees and the future of the agency. . . . We are in a time of uncertainty and high anxiety. The seemingly irrational General Fund cuts of 47% in 1980 are shocking." State government had always seemed like a very stable employer. No one could remember a time when such longtime employees had been reassigned or laid off. More than one hundred Forest Management Division employees were affected by the budget difficulties of 1980–81, and the number would have been higher had not a fairly substantial number of DNR employees chosen to sign up for "voluntary lay-off days." Employees could work nine days every two weeks, forgoing 10 percent of their salary and thereby reducing the number of layoffs.

Governor William G. Milliken imposed an April 1981 hiring freeze that applied even to temporary help, which meant that seedlings in the state nurseries could not be dug up or planted. Fortunately, the economic situation was less severe in neighboring states, and most of the trees were sold in bulk to Wisconsin and Minnesota. A small number of volunteer efforts resulted in the planting of a few trees in the Michigan state forests in the spring of 1981, but the net effect was slight.

TIMBER SALE PROCEDURES WERE ABBREVIATED AS A PART OF THE MOVE-ment to economize. Leading this effort was Dr. Nemah G. Hussain, a forest entomologist who joined the division in 1977 as the leader of the operations inventory system for the Upper Peninsula. In 1979, Webster moved Hussain to Lansing to take advantage of his computer knowledge and skills, putting him in charge of the fiscal aspects of the timber sale program. Most of his responsibilities involved the paperwork associated with timber sales. The state had always prided itself on its concise timber contract—one page, two-sided—but the process still had a lot of room for improvement. Under the old system, secretaries in the field first typed the sale proposal and sent it to Lansing. After the sale was approved, Lansing secretaries copied the information into the prospectus and sent it out for bids. Field secretaries copied the same information yet another time when the contract was issued. Hussain automated the whole system into one smooth stream so that the legal and technical language needed to be typed only once.

Changing the timber sale process seems quite simple when viewed in retrospect, but at the time the effort was beset by one difficulty after another. Austerity cutbacks made contracting difficult, and in-house personnel were not available to develop the needed computer programs. Some field offices had inadequate telephone service for good computer connections. Many field offices had only one computer, causing a bottleneck as people waited to enter their data. Many field employees were not comfortable with computers and resisted the changes. Nevertheless, the new system eventually became institutionalized. .

By this time, the sale of timber from state forestlands took place almost entirely through sealed bids at public auction because timber policy required advertisement of any sale in which two or more people could be expected to be interested. Interest in nearly everything the state forests had to offer remained high. The Lansing office mailed notices to newspapers and individuals who had requested them. Payment occurred in advance—10 percent down at the time of signing of the contract, with the balance due before cutting began. This procedure saved time for the foresters and technicians in comparison to the old way of scaling wood in the mill yard or the woods, keeping track of railroad car numbers, and chasing after stumpage payments. It also assured payment and helped prevent theft.

In addition to the streamlining of office and payment procedures connected with the timber sales, Hussain recommended shortcuts in the statistical sampling procedures used in the field examination and estimation of timber. Thus, timber management activities remained at reasonably high levels in spite of the reduction in staffing. Timber management had become increasingly important as an ever greater share of the Forest Management Division's budget was derived from revenue from land management, especially timber.

WITH ALL THE TURMOIL CAUSED BY BUDGET CUTS AND LAYOFFS, WEBSTER never lost his focus on improving the management of the state forests. He saw the forests as an important component of the economic diversity that Michigan sorely needed. Between 1980 and 1983, he guided the crafting of a Statewide Forest Resources Plan that emphasized both the economic and the recreational potential of all of Michigan's forestlands.

In September 1980, Milliken convened the Governor's Conference on Forest Resources, which yielded three sets of "major recommendations": improving the business climate for the forest industry; assuring a future supply of timber; and fully coordinating public and private forestry activities.[18]

Michigan's forest resources were maturing, a development that did not go unnoticed. In 1983, Governor James J. Blanchard named forest products as one of his "target industries" for growth and expansion. At about the same time, several major industry expansions were announced, including Weyerhaeuser's plan to build a plant at Grayling, Mead's plan to expand its paper mill at Escanaba, and Champion International's plan to build a new pulp and paper mill at Quinnesec. In addition, Champion International was producing steam from wood chips at its Gaylord plant, and at Midland, Dow-Corning was constructing a system to use chips for cogeneration. All of these projects focused on the overabundance of low-value hardwoods in need of thinning.

Webster had additional ideas on ways the state forests could assist in the expansion of the forest products industry. One of these was what he called timber volume agreements, under which the state would guarantee a company that built a major new wood-using plant or made major expansion of an existing plant the right to meet any bids for a certain portion of the state's surplus timber. This idea, proposed in 1984, did not enjoy a warm reception—from key legislators, from state forest managers, or from the industry—and disappeared by the end of that year.[19] Similarly, Senate Bill 501 of 1984 proposed leasing state forestlands to industry and making the lessee responsible for land management activities, including reforestation. This proposal, too, met with a cool reception and went nowhere.[20]

A more successful idea, first mentioned in 1984, was what came to be known as the Forest Development Fund. Economic analyses had shown that sound investments in timber management in the state forests could more than pay for themselves. Webster proposed that if the DNR could not get state appropriations to make the needed investments in timber management, it should borrow the money and pay it back with interest at the time of harvest. This idea intrigued a lot of people and gradually gained support within the department. Webster and Lansing staffer Ronald Murray presented the idea to the commission in July 1988. Credit was given to the Governor's Cabinet Council; First of Michigan Corporation, Detroit; and the legal firm of Miller, Canfield, Paddock, and Stone, also of Detroit, for their support in the development of a proposal for selling bonds to fund timber investments on state forest land. The commission listened, raised concerns regarding how land uses would be balanced, and then gave permission for the Forest Management Division to proceed with work on enabling legislation.[21] In addition to paying for needed silvicultural work on the state forests, this proposal offered the DNR's funding increased protection from raids by the governor or legislature. Bond proceeds would be protected by federal law and would be less vulnerable than the current Forest Management Fund.

A FRUSTRATION DEVELOPED AMONG THOSE ASSIGNED TO THE NEW SPE-
cialist positions at the state forest headquarters over a lack of specifics regarding their jobs and responsibilities. This frustration was most acute
among the planners, who seemed to have no responsibilities because no
formal planning process had been established. Their job evolved into leadership of the operations inventory procedures, schedules, and policies. This
arrangement came to work very well and resulted in a form of management
planning that included effective public participation.

Because the operations inventory examined 10 percent of the compartments in each forest each year, no forest would ever have up-to-date information for the whole district. Every year, each forest area held a
compartment review—a meeting of representatives of all DNR divisions in
which staff reviewed Forest Management Division staffers' prescriptions
for the compartments to be "entered" during the coming year. Compartments were randomly distributed around each forest area and varied in size,
averaging around fifteen hundred acres. Activities scheduled during the
"year of entry" might include thinning, harvest, planting, opening maintenance, trail construction, and many others. A typical compartment review
would consider prescriptions on ten to twenty compartments.

After Forest Management, the Wildlife Division was the most active in
the compartment review process. Department policy made the two divisions comanagers with equal say in management decisions, so Wildlife Division staff needed to be involved in every compartment. Biologists or other
Wildlife personnel often would take responsibility to do the field review on
one or two compartments and bring their recommendations to the review.
Fisheries Division biologists often commented on the need for shade or
sunlight on certain streams to regulate water temperature. Conservation
officers might be concerned about how road configurations would affect illegal hunting activity.

As the system evolved, notices of the compartment reviews appeared in
newspapers, and the public was invited to participate. In some cases, open
houses were held prior to compartment reviews to allow members of the
public a chance to talk informally to the various forest managers. These
meetings often resulted in some alterations in the prescriptions. Through
this process, the Forest Management Division kept a finger on the pulse of

public opinion and had an opportunity to mold those concerns into the management planning early enough to avoid confrontations.

Some confrontations did occur, however, causing state forest personnel considerable heartburn. One such confrontation occurred in response to an aspen clear-cut in Gladwin County. Some local residents drove by the site daily and were not placated by assurances that new aspens would sprout up during the first year and would soon cover the site. One resident appeared at several commission meetings to complain about the sale until Webster offered to donate some pine seedlings and a couple of his staffers to help direct a planting bee.[22] The pines were planted but were soon swallowed up by the vigorous young aspens. Similar crises popped up from time to time but became less frequent as the compartment review process matured and public involvement opportunity became more formalized.

While the overall planning effort on the state forests was continuing one compartment at a time, certain areas with special or unusual natural attributes received more concentrated attention. Special plans were devised for the Sand Lakes Quiet Area in Grand Traverse and Kalkaska Counties in 1972; the Jordan River Valley in 1975; the Mason Tract, a fifteen-hundred-acre tract along the Au Sable River, in 1978; Little Presque Isle on the Lake Superior shore near Marquette in 1981; Green Timbers Ranch, sixty-four hundred acres adjacent to the Pigeon River Country State Forest, in 1982; and Lime Island in the St. Mary's River in 1986. These and other such projects attested to the fact that the state forests were being managed for a much broader range of uses than simply timber.

INTERESTING DEVELOPMENTS IN WILDLIFE MANAGEMENT IN THE 1980S affected state forests. The pine marten and fisher, members of the weasel family dependent on mature forest habitat, were seen in Michigan for the first time in more than half a century. Both had been driven out of the state by the changes in habitat following the heavy logging of the late nineteenth century; both were reintroduced into the Upper Peninsula and found the habitat to their liking. Also, the Wildlife Division reintroduced moose to the Upper Peninsula through a deal struck with the Ontario Ministry of Natural Resources. This effort, too, succeeded. These reintroductions of species whose habitat requirements included mature forests provided further testimony to the recovery of the forests of northern Michigan.

In addition to wildlife species reintroduced to northern Michigan, others showed up on their own as the ecological pendulum swung back to forest cover. Timber wolves were seen occasionally, and sporadic reports of cougar sightings occurred. Wolf sightings were accepted as another indication of the forests' recovery, but cougar sightings were seen in a totally different light—more like UFO or Elvis sightings. Anyone who saw a mystery cat was a sure target of ridicule. When DNR silviculturist Michael Zuidema from Escanaba reported seeing a cougar, however, he countered the ridicule by launching an effort to collect information from observers all over the Upper Peninsula. This controversy continues to this day with biologists on either side of the issue although most biologists are very reluctant to acknowledge the existence of cougars in Michigan.

TREE PLANTING ON THE STATE FORESTS HAD HIT A LOW OF 340,000 TREES in 1976, partly because nearly all of the openings to be reforested had been planted and partly because DNR nursery policy gave priority to private lands for placement of nursery stock. The nursery policy had made it difficult for foresters in the field to plan planting programs, since availability of planting stock was not determined until midwinter, when orders from private landowners tapered off. Only then would foresters learn how many and what kind of trees they would be planting. Planting equipment was typically buried in snow at that time of year, delaying preparation time. The policy had outlived its usefulness and needed to be updated. Although the old openings, which were the easy planting sites, had been planted, the practice of clear-cutting in jack pine was resulting in a new, tougher class of planting sites filled with stumps, branches, and tops from the harvested trees. The Forest Cultivation program provided funds to purchase from Whitfield Manufacturing of Mableton, Georgia, planting machines sturdy enough to plant these new sites. The new machines had a steel enclosure that offered operators protection from sticks and branches, and the machines could split and plant through fresh pine stumps. A plow designed by Harry Tabor of Forestry Equipment Sales of Starkville, Mississippi, was added to the front of the bulldozer that pulled the planter. The plow scraped a three-foot-wide swath free of sticks and debris for the planter, thus allowing the planter's packing wheels to firm the earth around the seedlings. At times, a dozen of these machine combinations worked simultaneously across the state.

Rounding out the reforestation program under the new policy, which put priority on the needs of the state forests, was a change in the use of the Southern Michigan Nursery property. In 1981, Webster detailed a committee to study the DNR's nursery program: the committee concluded that the state no longer needed to sell seedlings to the public. The Christmas tree industry had led to development of a large number of private seedling nurseries with a high degree of technical competence. The committee recommended the closure of the Southern Michigan Nursery as a seedling production facility but suggested that it would make a good facility for production of genetically superior tree seeds in an orchardlike setting. Dr. Jonathan Wright and Dr. James Hanover of Michigan State University, both forest geneticists, had recommended seed orchards. Research had identified preferred sources of jack pine seed that would develop trees of better form and with faster growth than the average Michigan sources. A site in southern Michigan was considered ideal because of the longer growing season and the reduced chance of late frosts that would ruin the seed crop. The Southern Michigan Nursery site was a good fit on all counts.

The last crop of seedlings was shipped from the Southern Michigan Nursery in the spring of 1984, and in 1985 the first seed orchard was planted. The first orchard planted was European larch and was established in cooperation with the Institute of Paper Chemistry, located in Appleton, Wisconsin. Several years later, a jack pine orchard was planted. As the state forest centennial year arrived, both orchards were yielding significant amounts of seed.

One planting project worthy of note was the special plantations established in 1987 in honor of Michigan's 150th anniversary. At least three such plantations were created: one is visible along U.S. Highway 2 in Schoolcraft County, a few miles west of Thompson. Two others—near Gwinn and Cadillac—included the number 150 spelled out in rows of trees. The one near Gwinn used European larch in the middle of a red pine stand; the one near Cadillac used rows of red pine in an open area.

While most DNR employees were celebrating the state's sesquicentennial with tree planting, one did not take part. Forest fire officers had been investigating suspicious wildfires in the eastern Upper Peninsula for a few years and finally discovered that the perpetrator was a department employee who had always had a reputation for strongly opposing the planting of pines—ostensibly because the plantations detracted from the already dwindling habitat for sharptail grouse. He was convicted of arson and spent time in jail for setting fires on state forestland.

In the fall of 1987, the Wyman Nursery at Manistique suffered the loss of its main packing building and warehouse and its office building in two separate arson fires, cases in which no one was ever charged. A new building was constructed with an office, seedling packing facility, and walk-in cooler. Most people involved would say the net effect of the fires was an improvement, but none would recommend this method of getting a new building.

THE FOREST MANAGEMENT DIVISION NEVER RECOVERED ALL THE PEOPLE laid off in 1980–81. To make matters worse, the state offered an early retirement program in 1984, leading to the departure of more staff, only one in four of whom could be replaced regardless of whether the budget contained money for the position.[23] These reductions in staffing soon were felt outside as well as inside the department.

In October 1984, a number of specialty mills complained to the Natural Resources Commission that the Forest Management Division was not offering enough red pine poles for sale. The foresters' prescriptions recommended more poles than were being offered, but staffing reductions had hampered the state forest managers' ability to complete the fieldwork and paperwork.[24]

This criticism that the state was not offering enough timber for sale reappeared repeatedly in the years to come. It put division managers in the awkward position of encouraging the increased sale of timber—not because of pressure from the forest industry or because of a need for revenue but because the stand examinations and prescriptions written by forest staff said these treatments were needed to maintain the health and vigor of the state forests. In response, some forest managers began to adjust their prescriptions to more closely match their ability to accomplish the work. Word from Lansing clarified that all needed work should continue to be prescribed, but the controversy continued.

OTHER INTERESTING ISSUES DURING WEBSTER'S TENURE INCLUDED THE fencing and capping of old mines, the closing of small local dumps on state land, the establishment of the U.S. Navy's project ELF, and groundwater contamination in the Pigeon River Country State Forest from oil and gas brine pits, among others.

Project ELF had been around under various names (Project Sanguine and Project Seafarer) for nearly twenty years before it was built in the central Upper Peninsula and northern Wisconsin in the mid-1980s. The project involved a grid of underground antennas designed to communicate with submarines around the world. Opponents feared that the extreme low frequency (ELF) transmissions would cause damage to humans and wildlife, but pleas to the Natural Resources Commission went unanswered, and the system became operational in 1989, after the foresters at Gwinn, Ishpeming, and Escanaba had expended considerable time and energy clearing the rights-of-way for construction of the grid. The navy officially decommissioned the system in September 2004 as a consequence of improvements in communications technology, and complete removal is anticipated by 2007.[25]

OVER TIME, THE STATE FORESTS PROVIDED THE UNDERPINNING OF A significant expansion of the forest industry in Michigan. Representatives of the Weyerhaeuser Corporation were said to have commented that the state forests made the difference in their decision to build their plant at Grayling. Never before had they built a plant where they did not own a significant amount of forestland. They were confident that they could procure enough raw materials from the state through competitive bidding to take the place of company land. This was just what Filibert Roth, William Beal, Charles W. Garfield, Marcus Schaaf, and other forestry pioneers had foreseen—state forests supplying the framework for a renewed forest products industry.

In 1990, Hank Webster left the Michigan DNR for a position with the Lake States Forestry Alliance in St. Paul, Minnesota, bringing to a close another chapter of state forest history and setting the scene for some surprises in the final decade of the first century of Michigan's state forests.

Ecosystem Management and Biodiversity

1991–2005

In July 1990, following Hank Webster's departure, Donald Grant was appointed as acting head of the Forest Management Division while a permanent occupant was sought for the office. Grant lacked formal training as a professional forester but had extensive experience in forest fire control and was known to be a skillful administrator. He had previously served as Webster's assistant for field operations for forest management, fire control, and forest recreation and had a thorough understanding of the state forest system.

Grant served as interim chief until Gerald Thiede was appointed division chief and state forester in March 1991. "Those were tough times," Thiede recalled. "The department was in turmoil over budgets and reorganization rumors. The environmental divisions wanted a more centralized organization; the resource divisions wanted the opposite. Division chiefs were not permitted to have assistants. The new responsibilities, budget shortfalls, and attempts at reorganization were all-consuming."[1]

Thiede went on to describe some of the difficulties encountered during his first years as chief. This was a time of austerity as a result of a serious shortfall in the state budget, and raids on the Forest Management Fund were occurring. The fund was intended only for the management of the state forests, but its effectiveness was depleted in various ways, however inadvertently. One was the transfer of secretaries on paper from the Forest Management Division to a central pool. Funds were transferred to continue to support the positions. Then, when budget cuts occurred, secretaries were laid off, leaving the state forests without the secretaries, the authorized positions, or the money to hire or retain needed employees.

Another example was the transfer of title to an entire fleet of vehicles purchased by the Forest Management Fund for state forest use. To create a self-sustaining motor pool within the Department of Management and Budget, newly purchased vehicles were transferred to the new motor pool, and only partial reimbursement was made to the department that had purchased them. That department was then required to pay mileage and rental fees for use of those vehicles.

In November 1991, Michigan Governor John Engler signed four executive orders reorganizing the Department of Natural Resources (DNR). The governor eliminated nineteen boards and commissions, and the chair of the Natural Resources Commission became a gubernatorial appointee. (The commission previously had elected its chair each year). The commission retained the authority to select the director of the department, who was given authority to issue all permits and operating licenses formerly issued by such abolished bodies as the Water Resources Commission and the Air Pollution Control Commission. The governor also called for the codification of natural resources and environmental laws.[2]

Webster had initiated the Forest Development Fund during the 1980s with the idea of borrowing money through the sale of revenue bonds and using that money as an investment in timber production on state forestland. Returns from the timber investments would enable the loans to be repaid with interest, and since federal law would protect bond proceeds from any other use than that specified at the time of the bond sale, the fund could not be raided for other projects. All of the money in the fund would have to be spent on managing the state forests. This approach would indeed have constituted a great step forward in establishment of consistent budgets for forest management, but the fact that the fund could not be raided may have forestalled implementation of the bond sale by making legislators and department leaders reluctant to back the idea.

The department listed the implementation of the Forest Development Fund as one of two forestry priorities (along with completion of the Escanaba River State Forest plan) in 1991.[3] Ron Murray, in the Lansing office, developed long lists of forest treatments, such as thinning, planting, and release of crop trees and their anticipated rates of return based on the quality of the sites on which the trees were growing. Foresters in the field identified potential investments as they examined forest stands during the operations inventory procedure. Both biologists and foresters needed reassurance that none of these activities was new—they would continue with the same forest management procedures; only the source of the funding would change. But progress on the fund encountered one challenge after another, and budgetary confusion continued. In the face of all these challenges, the old issues of the 1980s continued to demand attention.

Rules for the use of off-road vehicles had not yet been finalized. A trail system had to be established and approved before any regulations could be enforced. In April 1991, commission member Gordon Guyer commended the DNR for having accomplished the trail development within tight time constraints.[4] Many people, including some foresters, disagreed with the presence of off-road vehicles on state lands, believing that the intrusion of these vehicles into the state forests would work against ecological recovery. While discussions of this nature took place, signs of the maturing and recovery of the forests continued to emerge.

The Region I report to the commission in February 1991 cited the "successful translocation of fisher" to the Upper Peninsula. The fisher, a member of the weasel family, was considered an indicator of mature forests, and observers hailed the animal's return as a strong indication of forest recovery. The decline in the fisher population had been linked to overtrapping, but its habitat requirements included a dense canopy forest. Wolves were also becoming established in the Upper Peninsula, having moved in from

Wisconsin and Ontario.[5] The vision of a restored ecosystem clearly was nearing fruition. The pieces were coming back together after having been separated for more than a century.

From their inception, a hallmark of the management of the state forests has been the planning that went into all aspects of the management. During this period, state forest planning became a concept, following activities occurring on the national forests throughout the country. This "new" planning continued on a pilot basis on the Pere Marquette and Escanaba River State Forests. In July 1991 a draft plan for the Escanaba River State Forest was announced to the commission, with a detailed presentation to be scheduled later.[6] Controversy followed on the heels of this announcement.

One of the provisions in the Escanaba River plan that raised public outcry was a proposed campground at Little Presque Isle, on the Lake Superior shore north of Marquette. This tract had been acquired from the Cleveland-Cliffs Iron Company and included a picturesque stand of hundred-year-old red pine and a beautiful sandy beach. Local residents picnicked and held parties there and did not take kindly to the idea of construction of a campground that would draw hosts of outsiders. The Forest Management Division took the idea back to the drawing board and formed an advisory committee in the fall of 1992 to do further study.[7] The committee issued its report the following May, and the planning team changed the Escanaba River forest plan accordingly.[8] The plan to build a campground was dropped in favor of a small parking lot for day users. Farther away from Lake Superior, six cabins were built on the west side of County Road 550—five on Harlow Lake and the sixth on the north side of Harlow Creek. They rent by the week, are very popular, and are the only cabins built for recreational use in the state forest system.[9]

At about the same time as the Little Presque Isle controversy, the Lake Superior State Forest was developing a plan for a small island in the St. Mary's River. Lime Island had been a refueling station for Great Lakes freighters; the Consolidated Coal Company of Cleveland, Ohio had donated the island to the state in 1982. Largely because of the remnants of the refueling station, DNR staffers thought that the island had little potential for recreational or any other use until Director Gordon Guyer requested an evaluation in 1986. The evaluation discovered ruins of lime kilns from the late nineteenth century and even earlier. The state archaeologist was notified, and a subsequent thorough study revealed remains of a sawmill from an undetermined era and a prehistoric Indian campsite.[10]

A modified campground design was proposed for Lime Island using houses in a tiny village formerly connected to the refueling station. The idea was controversial. Some forest managers worried that the distance from the shore to the island (2.5 miles) posed a serious impediment to maintenance of any island facilities. Forest Management Division staffer Dean Sandell envisioned Lime Island as a stopping point along a "water trail" on the St. Mary's River. Travelers in sea kayaks or other craft could stop at various islands along this trail; Lime Island's historic sites might be a focal point.[11]

In spite of the various misgivings, a plan was developed and approved, and open houses were held on the island in August 1992 and August 1994.[12] Today, Lime Island is a designated state forest campground with the village houses available for rent. Tent camping is available in a grassy area or on constructed tent platforms. A host couple spend the summer on the island, usually from May to October.[13]

Also emerging in 1992 was the issue of old-growth forest conservation, a subject that would command an immense amount of attention in the ensuing years. In August of that year, the department's deputy director, Michael D. Moore, proposed an addendum to the Statewide Forest Resources Plan to include the old-growth concept and to draft a policy.[14] Most foresters favored Moore's proposal, interpreting it to mean that any remaining patches of old-growth timber would be saved. Few such stands still existed, and wherever they could be found, some justification could be found in saving them as areas for ecological study. As work commenced on the policy, however, it became apparent that not everyone with an interest in old-growth forests shared the same concept of what they were or why they should be preserved.

Some old-growth proponents wanted to see special status conferred on stands that merely resembled true old growth or that might become old growth if left to become overmature. A large part of the rationale was a concern for endangered species that might be harmed by forest management activities. And while no such endangered species were known to inhabit most forest types, concern was expressed for species as yet undiscovered. Other concerns included the need for corridors for wildlife movement and a perceived need for stands that mirrored the conditions that prevailed when European settlers first arrived. Others argued that these stands—which are not truly old growth but merely resemble it—are the result of decades of management, especially in the case of northern hardwoods. The old-growth proposal seemed to be aimed at taking out of the foresters' hands the same tools that had brought about the desired conditions.

Proponents pointed out the small percentage of state forestland dedicated to old growth, a position that failed to consider those lands already transferred to state parks because of their old-growth characteristics. "Potential old growth" became a common recommendation forwarded by individuals at compartment reviews. A great deal of energy was spent arguing the relative merits and needs of old growth at a time when energy and staffing were at a premium.

In February 1993, DNR director Roland Harmes presented a department restructuring plan to the commission. The new plan would eliminate the regional offices, consolidate the field offices, and rename the districts "zones."[15] Harmes's idea seemed universally unpopular. Commission member David Holli of Ishpeming expressed concern over the pending loss of thirteen positions from the Forest Management Division.[16] Tom Washington, executive director of the Michigan United Conservation Clubs, appeared at a March meeting to urge the commission to table the plan. Washington said that it was hard to find support either inside or outside the DNR for this restructuring and described the reasoning behind it as "unclear."[17]

Harmes went ahead with the plan, and in 1995 the regions disappeared as a part of the DNR's administrative structure, although the offices at Roscommon and Marquette were kept open as department service centers. It quickly became clear, however, that the department needed to maintain an administrative presence outside of Lansing, and Edward (Ned) Caveney, former regional forester at Roscommon, was named field coordinator and added to the Lansing staff, although he remained physically located at Roscommon. Soon thereafter, Michael Paluda, former regional forester at Marquette, assumed a position as Forest Resource Protection Section Leader. Even though the regions were officially eliminated and the term was banished, they never really went away. Perhaps the most significant aspect of the restructuring was the closing of several field offices throughout the state.

Reduced budgets meant reduced staffing, and reduced staffing meant that tasks remained undone. Shortcuts had been developed in timber management procedures ten years earlier, and some additional procedural changes were now proposed, such as requiring timber purchasers to select trees for harvest and to take care of reforestation. These changes were not considered desirable or practical.

With the reduced staffing levels, state forest employees found it impossible to keep up with campground maintenance. This was more than a cosmetic concern with picking up litter: it was primarily an issue of public health. For example, employees lacked the time to do the required monthly testing of the water at campground wells; some campgrounds therefore were closed so that others could be kept safe for public use.[18] A cost analysis was done to identify those campgrounds receiving the least amount of use for the effort expended to keep them open, and twenty-three little-used and out-of-the-way campgrounds were subsequently closed.[19] This action represented a de facto shift in state forest recreation policy away from wilderness camping and toward a more concentrated format. Relatively few people had used the closed campgrounds, so relatively few mourned their passing. Yet they had once been the essence of the camping program. Local units of government took over management of some of the closed campgrounds, such as the Healy Lake State Forest Campground in Manistee County, which is presently administered by Springdale Township.

Outside groups occasionally would offer help to the managers of the state forests in the form of either free labor or monetary donations. Following the successful example of the North Carolina Department of Transportation's Adopt-a-Highway program, DNR employee Virginia Pierce, district waste management supervisor, began an Adopt-a-Forest program in 1989 in which volunteers could help clean up junk dumped on state forestland. The Adopt-a-Forest program quickly expanded from Roscommon County to the entire Au Sable State Forest, and in 1991 it went statewide, including all public lands. Strong industrial support was received from Consumers Power Company and Michigan Consolidated Gas Company as well as the Michigan Forest Resource Alliance, which serves as a tax-exempt umbrella group allowing tax-deductible gifts to Adopt-a-Forest. The program boasts a corps of eight thousand volunteers and has cleaned a million acres of public land.[20]

The Forest Management Division's Lansing office staff began a State Forest Family program to encourage and handle monetary gifts. In addition to the various individual memorial gifts, two notable corporate donors emerged: Elton Black Funeral Homes in southeast Michigan and Kinko's donated several thousand dollars each for reforestation.[21] Both corporations were users of wood and wood products (although in quite different ways), and both wanted to give something back. This program remains in operation.

Detroit Edison Company also provided contributions for reforestation based on a need to counteract carbon emissions from the company's power plants. The U.S. Environmental Protection Agency offered Detroit Edison credit if the company would underwrite the planting of enough trees to sequester an equivalent amount of carbon to what Detroit Edison's power plants were emitting. Millions of trees were planted with this funding.

FOR MANY YEARS, VOLUNTEER CAMPGROUND HOSTS HAVE WORKED AT larger state forest campgrounds during the summer months. The hosts assist campers in a variety of ways—answering questions about the local area, arranging campground activities, and representing the DNR in the campground. They must provide their own camping units and equipment and must be at least eighteen years of age. Volunteer programs have become so important in management of the state forests that a position has been established in the division to coordinate such activities.[22]

In 1994 the planning experiment reached a close with the completion of a second state forest plan, this one for the Pere Marquette in the northern Lower Peninsula. The two state forest plans had different processes and procedures, and at the outset, the idea had been to learn from these pilot projects and to use that knowledge to craft a process by which plans would be written for the other four forests. But the plans took more time than anticipated to reach completion and had less impact than anticipated. When reduced staffing was factored into the equation, continuing seemed neither possible nor practical. Plans for the Copper Country, Lake Superior, Mackinaw, and Au Sable State Forests were never started.[23] Those forests without formal plans devised procedures for public participation in their manage-ment. In general, the forest areas held open houses at which public com-ments were solicited on management activities planned for the coming year. These open houses usually preceded the more formal compartment re-views by a few days.

At the first commission meeting following release of the Pere Mar-quette State Forest plan, a representative of the Sierra Club voiced opposi-tion to nearly every aspect of both the Escanaba River and Pere Marquette plans. Specifically, he objected to what he termed the "demand-based" na-ture of the plans and the key-value approach to management as well as their treatment of biological diversity and old growth.[24] Shortly thereafter, the Sierra Club protested to the Natural Resources Commission regarding two state forest timber sales in Emmet County on the Mackinaw State Forest, demanding time to review the sales before contracts were issued, even though bids had already been opened. In fact, the Sierra Club requested a contested case hearing in front of the commission. The commission denied this request based on the fact that the Forest Management Division had provided interested parties an opportunity to fully participate in the process and urged the department to proceed with the sales.[25] The case, gen-erally referred to as the Wycamp Oaks and Wycamp II timber sales, resulted in the Sierra Club filing a lawsuit on June 15, 1994. Ingham County Circuit Court Judge William Collette issued a temporary restraining order, blocking harvest for two weeks. He also issued a preliminary injunction that pre-vented the timber from being cut under the purchase contracts. On Febru-ary 15, 1995, however, Collette lifted the preliminary injunction, writing in his opinion that the "Sierra Club participated in every stage of the delibera-tive process allowed by the DNR. The DNR decided in favor of selling the timber."[26] In the end, the timber was harvested, and the scientific forest management of the properties continued.

IN 1995 THE NATURAL RESOURCES COMMISSION APPROVED A NEW RECRE-ational initiative on which the Forest Management Division had been work-ing for three years. The five-point plan, Forest Recreation 2000—A Strategic Plan for Michigan's State Forest Recreation System, was prepared under the leadership of division section head Hector Chiunti by a citizen advisory committee chaired by David Smethurst of Gaylord. The advisory committee was created by statute in 1990 following the proposed closure of almost one-third of the state forest campgrounds. The committee included representatives of many interest and user groups, including trail users, mountain bikers, canoeists, snowmobilers, and wilderness advocates. The draft plan was reviewed and discussed in early 1995 at nine public informational hearings attended by more than five hundred citizens. The strategic plan included a forest recreation vision and five major points for action that required commitments from the DNR, legislature, voters, the Departments of Transportation and Civil Service, and the Travel Bureau: (1) a commitment to high-quality nationally recognized forest recreation programs; (2) a commitment to renovate existing facilities through a bond program; (3) a commitment to provide proper resources to manage the system; (4) a commitment to provide appropriate earmarked stable funding; and (5) a commitment to provide adequate public information.[27]

While the Lansing staff fought the battles of the budget, foresters and technicians in the field continued to do the work of managing the state forests—inventorying compartments, making prescriptions, holding compartment reviews, and carrying out the prescriptions. Inventories showed continuing increases in timber volume that led to increased prescriptions for timber sales. The quality increase that can be expected from good management began to reveal itself in higher bid prices for state timber. Other factors, such as supply and demand, no doubt also came to play as revenues from state forest timber sales rose to new heights through the early 1990s.

By fiscal year 1994, annual stumpage revenue had reached nearly $14 million.[28] The legislature withdrew the remaining General Fund support from the timber management program on the state forests, effectively making them self-supporting. Lansing staff had hoped to have the Forest Development Fund's revenue bonds sold before this happened, giving more assurance of steady funding, but bonds had not been sold, and the increasing timber revenue weakened the argument for continued pursuit of bonds.[29] A great deal of work had been done—enabling legislation had been passed, the old Forest Management Fund was replaced by the new Forest Development Fund, and a Forest Finance Authority Committee had been appointed as prescribed by the new law, but no bonds were ever sold. The Finance Authority met a few times, but no further action occurred.

∾ MICHIGAN STATE FOREST TIMBER SALES REVENUE

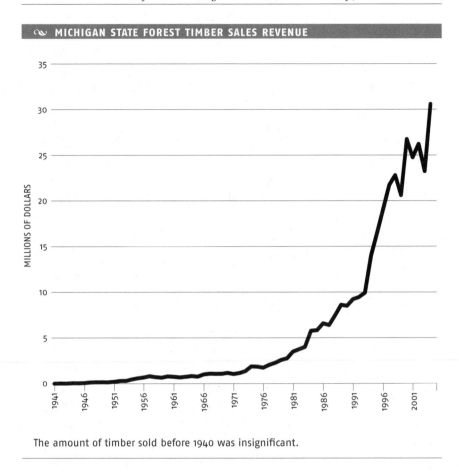

The amount of timber sold before 1940 was insignificant.

Instead of the independence that would be expected to result from the self-supporting status, the timber programs remained subject to the ups and downs of the state's budget. State government hiring freezes were applied to positions whose funding came through the Forest Development Fund even though ample money was on hand to pay for additional help. Instead, expensive contracts were entered with consulting firms, which then arranged timber sales based on compartment prescriptions. Satisfactory work was done in most cases, but when writing and administration of the contracts was considered, it was more expensive than doing the work with department employees had they been available.

Considerable controversy revolved around this topic of timber sales and contracting. Members of the forest products industry felt betrayed by the Forest Management Division, which they saw as reneging on an agreement to offer a certain volume of timber after receiving authority to hire new timber sale personnel, an action the industry had strongly supported. The Forest Management Division cited the need for time to train new employees and the press of other departmental responsibilities, particularly forest fire control, on employees' time. Industry representatives asked why, when employees paid out of the timber sale budget were sent out West to fight fires, the federal reimbursement money was not spent on additional help for timber sales.

The upshot was a weakening of the forest products industry's support for additional state timber employees. Perhaps to underscore their discontent, industry officials supported a state Senate boilerplate amendment to the DNR budget bill establishing a volume target for state forest timber sales in the 1997-98 fiscal year. The target was essentially equivalent to the previous year's sales, so it was not unreasonable, but this was the first time in the nearly one hundred years of state forest management that politicians had set prescription levels for timber management. Similar amendments have appeared in appropriations acts since then.

In late July 1995, Governor Engler issued an executive order creating the Department of Environmental Quality. The new department was to have its director appointed by the governor, and there would be no oversight committee such as the Natural Resources Commission involved in the new department's operation. Engler transferred most environmental responsibilities, including air- and water-quality programs, from the DNR to the new department; he also transferred the Geological Survey Division and the Land and Water Division. The reconfigured DNR contained most of the elements of the original Department of Conservation created in 1921. Shortly after this split, Harmes resigned as director. The Natural Resources Commission asked Michael D. Moore, a forester and the recently retired deputy director for resources, to return as director and to serve until a permanent director could be found.

In June 1997, foresters around the state were shocked to hear that K. L. Cool, who had taken over as DNR director from Moore in April 1996, had replaced Thiede as head of the Forest Management Division with Fisheries

Division chief John Robertson.[30] Thiede retained the title of state forester so that the state would continue to qualify for federal funds that required each state to have a professional forester with that title, but he was reassigned to a new Office of Field and Investigative Studies and had little further contact with the management of the state forests. Edward Hagan, a longtime DNR employee, was assigned to the Forest Management Division to provide special assistance to Robertson. Cool, a biologist with considerable experience in the western states, had little or no experience in the management of public lands.

Robertson, who was well liked as an administrator but claimed little knowledge of forestry or of the programs of the Forest Management Division, offered his first recorded comments to the commission as forestry chief in the spring of 1998 in response to a proposal to ban the use of the screw-in steps bow hunters often used to climb up to tree stands. Robertson, Cool, and Tim Karasek of the Michigan Association of Timbermen spoke against the use of these devices on state lands.[31] The steps posed a physical threat to anyone who harvested or processed trees containing them and degraded the value of the timber into which they were placed. Two state senators spoke in favor of allowing the steps to be used, arguing that they were fairly expensive and were not likely to be left in the trees. Forest industry representatives brought in damaged equipment as evidence that steps were indeed left in trees. Officials from Champion International spoke against the steps and promised to establish policies on Champion lands that would conform to the DNR policies.[32]

The debate culminated in a statement by Natural Resources Commission chair Keith Charters, who said "that when this was added to the agenda, he [would] have been willing to compromise on this theme and ban the use of screw in steps on state forest areas, but allow them on state game and recreation areas in southern Michigan. He changed his opinion due to an amendment in the Senate stating that if the [commission did] not approve the use of screw-in steps, the Legislature would take $1 million from the Forest Management budget. This amount was subsequently changed to $1. [Even so,] Chairman Charters said he [would] not sacrifice the integrity of the Commission." The commission then voted unanimously to ban the steps from all state lands.[33]

At the same time, the state forest road system was in poor shape. Ted Reuschel, staff forester in charge of forest operations, made a plea to the commission for better support for fixing the state forest road system—it was becoming a matter of public safety, he said.[34] A short-lived controversy over allowing sled dogs to use groomed snowmobile trails arose in December 1996.[35] An early retirement program took dozens of state forest employees in the first half of 1997 amid rumors of still more organizational change.

These concerns plus screw-in steps, bovine tuberculosis, deer damage to young trees, deer baiting, and old growth dominated the commission's forestry-related discussions during the 1990s and early twenty-first century. In 2000, the commission received several presentations regarding old-growth management. The definition of "old growth" seems to have evolved to include red and white pines over seventy-five years of age, which were declared to be of "global rarity."[36] According to that philosophy, all of the plantations established by the Civilian Conservation Corps should be declared old growth and off-limits to further thinning.

The forest industries criticized what they saw as the commission's lack of interest in forestry matters. A November 1999 presentation to the commission cited the lack of plans for education and public assistance for landowners as well as the failure to complete the Forest Development Fund bonding initiative.[37] The Natural Resources Commission's Policy Committee took up the subject of the Forest Development Fund, and in February 2001, Cool commented in a committee report that the fund was "volatile, unpredictable and influenced by global factors beyond DNR's control. The DNR relies on this Fund for management of forest and recreational activities. We, therefore, need to understand the Fund on both a local and global basis. Inaction is something the DNR cannot do."[38]

Robertson retired from state service in December 2000 and was replaced by acting chief Ed Hagan.[39] In the spring of 2001, Mindy Koch, another non-forester, was appointed permanently to the position of division chief. A longtime department employee, Koch had most recently served as head of the Land and Mineral Service Division. Her formal education was in resource development at Michigan State University.[40] Koch's appointment coincided with the addition to the division of the mineral management responsibilities of her former division, and the Forest Management Division was renamed the Forest, Mineral, and Fire Management Division. Once again, the state forests had to vie for attention not only with issues surrounding forest fire prevention and control but also with such major resource concerns as mineral leasing and gas storage. Former state forester Webster had likened a similar situation to "sharing the bathtub with a walrus."

At the turn of the new century foresters observed that certain lands contained timber of commercial value but had some limiting factors that might prevent prescribing harvest activities, at least for a time. Nearly 400,000 acres are reviewed each year to evaluate current forest conditions and to prescribe treatments including harvesting opportunities. Limiting factors are identified and can include such conditions as access problems, threatened and endangered species, recreational conflicts, or severe slope. These limiting factors are descriptions of on-the-ground conditions and are not used as decision rules. The use of the limiting factor concept highlights the need to find solutions to conditions at any problematic site.

In 2005, a geologist by training, Lynne Boyd was named chief of the division. Again, an individual with little experience in forest management was selected to guide the future of the state forests. Boyd has worked hard to gain acceptance of all of the employees of the division and all of the outside interest groups.

DURING THE 1980S, AN INTERNATIONAL CONCEPT OF FOREST CERTIFI-cation was developed. This concept involves an in-depth look at the forest management practices of requesting woodland managing organizations. It is administered by independent third-party auditing groups. Its purpose is to identify lands that are managed to meet agreed-upon standards. The underlying concept is to promote forest practices that are economically, environmentally, and socially sustainable. Once lands are certified, annual audits are generally required. Today some major timber-product users are requiring that the raw materials they buy be produced from certified forests. Certification may function someday as a market-based mechanism to reward superior forest management. A special label may identify products from certified forestland.

In February of 2004, Governor Jennifer Granholm called for certification of Michigan's State Forests during the 2004 Governors Forest Summit in Minnesota. Later that year the Michigan legislature enacted Public Act 125 of 2004 which stated, in part, that "the department shall seek and maintain third-party certification that the management of the state forest and other state owned lands owned or controlled by the department satisfies the sustainable forestry standards of at least 1 credible nonprofit, nongovernmental certification program". The DNR elected to seek certification under standards developed by both the Forest Stewardship Council and the Sustainable Forest Initiative, two third-party certification organizations.

Preliminary visits were conducted in 2004, followed by numerous internal audits to ensure that forest certification standards were being met in the state forest operations. Certification visits by both organizations took place in the fall of 2005. Following an exhaustive process both the Forest Stewardship Council and the Sustainable Forest Initiative certified the state forests of Michigan soon afterward.

When announcing this landmark certification, Governor Granholm noted that "Today marks an historic milestone in Michigan's forest management history. Dual certification affirms that our state-owned forests are managed in a healthy, sustainable way. It strengthens Michigan's economy, maintains our competitiveness in global timber markets and gives consumers confidence that they are buying and using products from well managed forests. Forest certification is a seal of approval for environmentally responsible wood and paper products. Michigan's vast state forests are a source of pride for our state, a source of jobs and a tourism magnet. I commend the DNR for the hard work they have done to achieve dual certification for our state forests."[41]

MICHIGAN'S STATE FORESTS HAVE GROWN IN AREA TO NEARLY 4 MILLION acres, larger than the state of Connecticut and three times the size of the state of Delaware. Michigan has the largest dedicated state forest system in the United States. The volume and value of the timber growing on these lands has steadily increased since they were dedicated as state forests. Management of these forestlands was intended to provide recreational opportunities for the people of Michigan and to restore the economic activity that was once connected with our forests.

It took fifty years to turn our once-productive forests into wastelands; it has taken a hundred years to build them back. Today, revenue from the controlled sale of timber from the state forests is sufficient to cover the costs of management. The same management that has guided the recovery of the forest has provided game habitat and has paved the way for the return of the moose, fisher, wolf, and marten, all of which were driven out when the forest was destroyed. These forests do not look artificial. Rather, they look so natural that some people regard them as wilderness and unknowingly seek to protect them from the foresters who manage them.

The recreation program on the state forests now includes 145 campgrounds, 1,500 miles of snowmobile trails, 2,325 miles of off-road-vehicle trails, and 655 miles of rail trails.[42] In addition, many hundreds of miles of riding-hiking trails and pathways wind around the state forests. Thousands of Michigan residents spend summer vacations and weekends throughout the year enjoying these facilities.

The visions of William Beal, Charles Garfield, Filibert Roth, Marcus Schaaf, and many others have become reality. Still, clouds gather overhead. Some groups continue to lobby for designation of state forests as wilderness or old growth; others push for the disposal of the lands. Still others would give management responsibilities to the forest industry.

A long-range vision was required to establish the state forests and to restore the forest resource. As that vision nears completion at the century mark, another is needed to take its place. The people of Michigan can be proud of what they have accomplished through careful management and stewardship of these lands for the past hundred years; with knowledge and understanding, even more can be expected in the future.

Epilogue

GREAT GAINS HAVE BEEN MADE IN THE PAST CENTURY IN RESTORING PRO-
ductivity to the once-abandoned lands that make up Michigan's state forests.
Timber productivity has increased from near zero to more than seven hundred thousand cords per year. Hunting, camping, and other recreational uses
have reached levels beyond the dreams of those who first conceived the idea
of this public forest system. Campgrounds, hiking trails, snowmobile trails,
and various other trails and facilities provide opportunities for hundreds of
thousands of users. Management revenues have reached an annual level of
$30 million. Surely the founders' vision has been realized.

But it seems that something has been lost as well. Is it possible that we
have come to take this great success story for granted? Has the zeal for
restoration been replaced by a routine management workload?

In the early years of the Department of Conservation, reforestation and
fire control were prominent topics at each of the Conservation Commission's

Michigan State Forests have provided untold hours of outdoor recreation to citizens and visitors for more than a century. Hunting, snowmobiling, bird watching, hiking, cross-country skiing, and camping are a few of these activities. Courtesy of the Michigan Department of Natural Resources.

monthly meetings. Today, the Department of Natural Resources gives little attention to the state forests; forestry-related topics rarely appear on the Natural Resources Commission's agenda. At one time, timber sales above a certain size required commission approval, but these, too, have gradually become routine. The commission delegated the approval authority to the director; the director delegated it to the chief of the division, and the chief delegated it to the Lansing forestry staff.

As a result of these gradual changes, commission members now are generally unfamiliar with the normal operation of the state forests. Department staffers periodically have offered commission members the opportunity to visit specific site locations to observe the modern aspects of forest management, but such chances occur all too infrequently. Something of the department's focus has been lost through this evolutionary process.

Another symptom of this loss of focus is in the naming system. In 2005, no tract bears the official title "state forest." Michigan has a state forest system composed of management units named for the town in which the forester's office is located. Although these are just names, something was lost when we went from the Fife Lake or the Lake Superior State Forest to the Cadillac or Newberry Forest Management Unit.

A long-range vision had been required to establish the state forests and to restore them to productivity. One after another leader shared that vision and carried it forward, each one recognizing and building on the work of his predecessors. Do we now consider the vision to have been fulfilled?

If portions of the vision have been lost at the top, what are the effects on the workers in the forests? Do the field employees remember the original mission? Do they understand that the pines they are thinning were planted by the Civilian Conservation Corps or that the hardwoods they are marking were clear-cut for charcoal before the state acquired the land? Do they still see themselves as a part of a restoration team? If not, a part of the vision has been blurred.

It is difficult to predict what future generations will want from their forests. Certification of Michigan's state forests has been granted by the Forest Stewardship Council and Sustainable Forest Initative. This process grants formal approval of sustainability and testifies to the professional forest management that has been applied over the past century. Forests in general serve many purposes—they produce oxygen and store carbon, provide habitat for a myriad of species, and protect soil from erosion. Regional and global climate is regulated in part by forests. Forests' role in protecting watersheds, supplying wood products, and providing places for recreation is certainly well documented. Michigan's state forests contribute to all of these purposes. The forest certification process details the sustainability of this magnificent state resource. Perhaps it will help rekindle the vision.

The state forestlands will likely become more important to the state's recreation and forest products industries. The industrial forestland ownership in Michigan (and indeed in the United States) is undergoing significant change. Timberland investment management organizations (TIMOs) are swiftly acquiring lands formerly held by integrated forest industry companies, companies that managed the forestland, harvested the timber, operated the mills, and sold the finished products. These integrated companies often were good corporate neighbors and community members, but the investment management organizations have primarily the goal of return on investment, with little vision of the long-range future, thereby increasing the pressure on the publicly owned lands to provide many of the other components of forestland use.

A substantial danger lurks with those who periodically promote converting portions of the state forests to private ownership. The exchange of properties surely often enhances management capability for both ownerships, but outright disposal of public lands makes little sense. Serious temporary state budget problems often drive these discussions. It makes as much sense for a farmer to sell his seed corn as it does for the state to engage in wholesale disposal of public lands.

Neil deGrasse Tyson, Frederick P. Rose Director of the Hayden Planetarium in New York City, wrote of our country's loss of focus on scientific centers of excellence, "Many factors influence how and why a nation will make its mark at a particular time in history. Strong leadership matters. So does access to resources. But something else must be present—something less tangible, but with the power to drive people to focus their emotional, cultural, and intellectual capital on creating islands of excellence in the world. On the blind assumption that things will continue forever as they are, people who live in such dynamic times often take the excellence for granted, leaving the nation's achievements susceptible to abandonment by the very forces that gave rise to them." Tyson cited the loss of the supercollider from the United States to Europe after Congress discontinued its funding in mid-construction.[1] New discoveries in nuclear physics will be made at the Large Hadron Collider, run by the European Laboratory for Particle Physics. We took our leadership role for granted—and lost it.

Our state forests have become islands of excellence in forest management. That was the vision of the founders. The people of Michigan can be proud of what they have accomplished through careful management and stewardship of these lands for the past hundred years. High-quality hardwoods have become a hallmark of Michigan's state forests, providing economic value and beauty unsurpassed by northern hardwoods anywhere in the world. Michigan's state forests provide more jack pine habitat for the rare Kirtland's warbler than any other ownership in the world. Magnificent red pine plantations are now reaching economic maturity, assisting the stability of northern Michigan's communities. These forests are truly world class. And who knows about them?

Have we slid into the situation Tyson describes in which we take excellence for granted? Are our state forests susceptible to abandonment, as was the supercollider? Evidence indicates that the answer to both questions is yes. Perhaps a new vision is needed to bring this truly remarkable story of recovery back into proper focus. Will we continue to apply our knowledge and improve our forest management skills? We have come a great distance in the past century; with knowledge and understanding, even more can be expected in the coming years. Challenges posed by conflicting uses, strained budgets, and exotic species will test our ability and resolve to manage these lands effectively. Will we rekindle and continue the vision? Or will we let it slip away?

What's in a Name?

THE STATE ORGANIZATION RESPONSIBLE FOR THE MANAGEMENT OF THE state forests has had a variety of names over the past hundred years. The (second) Michigan Forestry Commission was created in 1899 and was the agency in charge of the state forests (known as forest reserves) when they were originally established in 1903. In 1909 the Michigan Legislature passed Public Act 280, which created the Public Domain Commission. This constituted the state government's first attempt to combine the duties of natural resource agencies—that is, of the Michigan Forestry Commission and the commissioner of the State Land Office. Later, under Public Act 28 of 1915, the Public Domain Commission took on the duties of the state game, fish, and forestry warden.

When the Department of Conservation was formed (Public Act 17 of 1921), all duties related to conservation and protection of natural resources in state government were centralized in one organization. The department originally consisted of nine divisions: Game Protection and Propagation, Fish Cultural Operations, Forest Fire Control, Forestry and Silviculture, Public Lands, State Parks, Geology, Predatory Animal Control, and Education. The Forestry and Silviculture Division was renamed the Forestry Division shortly thereafter, around 1923.

In 1963–64, the division was renamed the Forestry Section in an attempt to rid the department of the organizational name "division" in response to the report from Governor George W. Romney's twenty-one-member citizens committee studying the Department of Conservation. Ralph MacMullan, the department director, said, "The old Department divisions, as such, have been dissolved. Taking their place in the Lansing office are sections, which have been relieved of responsibility for supervision of work in the field."[1] This effort was short-lived, and the name Forestry Division returned sometime in 1965.

The Executive Reorganization Act (Public Act 380 of 1965) transferred five commissions to the Department of Conservation: the State Waterways Commission, the Water Resources Commission, the Michigan Tourist Council, the Mackinac Island State Park Commission, and the Boating Control Commission. Shortly thereafter, Public Act 353 of 1968 created the Department of Natural Resources and transferred all duties from the Department of Conservation. Governor William G. Milliken issued Executive Orders 1973-2 and 1973-2a, transferring all environmental programs—including sewage system maintenance and certification, solid waste disposal, and licensing of septic tank cleaners—in the Department of Public Health to the Department of Natural Resources. Watershed management and drain code were transferred from the Department of Agriculture. The Water Resources Commission and the Air Pollution Control Commission were changed from Type I to Type II transfers, making both subordinate to the Natural Resources Commission. Finally, the executive order divided the department into two branches, natural resources and environmental protection, each with its own deputy and its own funding.

In 1975 Department of Natural Resources director Howard Tanner, with Natural Resources Commission approval, appointed a committee of twelve department employees to study the organization and make recommendations for change. Executive Order 1976-8 implemented the committee's suggested reorganization. The two-branch system was eliminated, and several bureaus were created to manage the divisions and offices. Contrary to the committee's recommendations, regional offices were limited in authority, and the department returned to a straight-line management style. In April 1977, the Forest Fire Division and the Forestry Division were combined to create the Forest Management Division. Executive Order 1991-31 subsequently reorganized and created a new Department of Natural Resources, an effort unanimously supported by the Michigan Supreme Court in September 1993.

Governor John Engler issued Executive Order 1995-18, effective October

1, 1995, which separated environmental and natural resources functions into two departments, elevating environmental protection to cabinet status for the first time in history. This changed the Department of Natural Resources back to much of the original Conservation Department focus from 1921, including outdoor recreation, wildlife and fisheries management, forest management, state lands and minerals, state parks and recreation areas, and conservation law enforcement.

The Forest Management Division remained in the Department of Natural Resources and was renamed the Forest, Mineral, and Fire Management Division on April 1, 2001, with the addition of certain functions of the Land and Mineral Services Division.

UNITS MANAGING MICHIGAN'S STATE FORESTS

- Michigan Forestry Commission, 1899–1909
- Michigan Public Domain Commission, 1909–21
- Forestry and Silviculture Division, Michigan Department of Conservation, 1921–23
- Forestry Division, Michigan Department of Conservation, 1923–63, 1965–68
- Forestry Section, Michigan Department of Conservation, 1963–65
- Forestry Division, Michigan Department of Natural Resources, 1968–1977
- Forest Management Division, Michigan Department of Natural Resources, 1977–2001
- Forest, Mineral, and Fire Management Division, Michigan Department of Natural Resources, 2001–

STATE FORESTERS

- Filibert Roth (state forest warden), September 23, 1903–June 30, 1909
- Marcus Schaaf, March 10, 1910–February 28, 1949
- George S. McIntire, March 1, 1949–January 14, 1961
- Theron E. (Ted) Daw, January 15, 1961–June 30, 1975
- Henry H. Webster, July 1, 1975–July 13, 1990

- Donald D. Grant (acting state forester), July 14, 1990–March 2, 1991
- Gerald J. Thiede (chief/state forester), March 3, 1991–June 30, 1997; (state forester), July 1, 1997–August 31, 2002
- Bernard Hubbard, September 1, 2002–June 4, 2005
- *Vacant*, June 5, 2005–

Division Chiefs Not Carrying the Title of State Forester

- John M. Robertson, July 1, 1997–April 15, 2000
- Edward J. Hagan (acting), April 16, 2000–April 13, 2001
- Arminda Koch, April 16, 2001–July 19, 2004
- Lynne Boyd, January 2, 2005–

Notes

PREFACE

1. Donald W. Floyd, *Forest Sustainability: The History, The Challenge, The Promise* (Durham, N.C.: Forest History Society, 2002), ix.

INTRODUCTION

1. Robert Wells, *Daylight in the Swamp* (Garden City, N.Y.: Doubleday, 1978), 34, 196.
2. Gifford Pinchot, *Breaking New Ground* (New York: Harcourt, Brace, 1947), 26.

CHAPTER 1. THE AWAKENING, 1888–1903

1. Michigan Board of Agriculture, *Annual Report*, 1888, 306–8.
2. Ibid., 307.
3. Ibid., 337.
4. One of Beal's other concerns was the control of weeds, such as quackgrass, which hampers crop production. His son-in-law, author Ray Stannard Baker, once remarked that Beal had "only three enemies in the world: alcohol, tobacco and quackgrass." Michael D. Moore and William B. Botti, *Michigan's Famous and Historic Trees* (Corunna, Mich.: Michigan Forest Association, 1976), 17.
5. William J. Beal to Charles A. Garfield, March 13, 1908, Garfield Papers, Bentley Historical Library, University of Michigan, Ann Arbor.
6. Michigan Board of Agriculture, *Annual Report*, 1889, 369.

7. Michigan Board of Agriculture, *Annual Report,*1893, 468, 470.

8. Michigan Board of Agriculture, *Annual Report*, 1888, 103–8.

9. Michigan Forestry Commission, background to minutes, State of Michigan Archives, Lansing.

10. Allen, *Michigan Log Marks*, 83.

11. George Fuller, *Messages of the Governors of Michigan* (Lansing: Michigan Historical Commission, 1925–27), 3.

12. Michigan Forestry Commission, background to minutes, State of Michigan Archives.

13. Charles W. Garfield, *The Wasteful West, Where the Timber Went: The Story of Giant Industry and a Gigantic Greed,* ca. 1905, Bentley Historical Library, University of Michigan, Ann Arbor.

14. Michigan Forestry Commission, minutes, September 30, 1899, State of Michigan Archives, Record group 60-19, Box 1.

15. Ibid., January 3, 1900.

16. Michigan Forestry Commission, *Annual Report*, 1900, 17.

17. Charles L. DeWaele to editor, *Crawford County Avalanche*, August 28, 1902.

18. *Crawford County Avalanche*, July 3, 1902.

19. Fred Janette, "Public Owns Tracts of Potential Forests," *Detroit News*, May 25, 1920, 1.

20. Michigan Forestry Commission, *Annual Report*, 1901, 5.

21. *Crawford County Avalanche*, January 2, 1902.

22. Michigan Forestry Commission, minutes, n.d. [June 6, 1902], State of Michigan Archives, Record group 60-19, Box 1.

23. Ibid., July 31, 1902.

24. Ibid., July 18, 1902.

25. Ibid., August 28, 1902.

26. "Michigan: Off the Tax Rolls and on Again," in *Forests and Forestry in the American States*, ed. Widner, 191.

27. Michigan Forestry Commission, minutes, April 8, 1903, State of Michigan Archives, Record group 60-19, Box 1.

CHAPTER 2. THE FOUNDATION, 1903–1907

1. Michigan Forestry Commission, minutes, July 16, 1903, State of Michigan Archives, Record group 60-19, Box 1.

2. Ibid., July 27, 1903.

3. G. H. Collingwood, "Filibert Roth: An Appreciation," *American Forests*, January 1926, 43; "Filibert Roth," Bentley Historical Library, University of Michigan, Ann Arbor.

4. Michigan Forestry Commission, minutes, July 27, 1903, State of Michigan

Archives, Record group 60-19, Box 1.

5. Ibid., September 25, 1903.

6. Ibid., December 5, 1903.

7. Ibid., February 25, 1904.

8. Ibid.

9. Ibid., April 22, 1904.

10. Charles W. Garfield to Gifford Pinchot, February 29, 1904, Garfield Papers, Bentley Historical Library, University of Michigan, Ann Arbor.

11. Michigan Forestry Commission, *Annual Report*, 1903–4, 24.

12. Ibid.

13. Ibid., 35, 39.

14. Ibid., 37.

15. Ibid., 39.

16. Michigan Forestry Commission, minutes, September 26, 1908, State of Michigan Archives, Record group 60-19, Box 1.

17. Mitchell and Robson, *Forest Fires and Forest Fire Control*, 21.

18. Michigan Forestry Commission, minutes, September 26, 1908, State of Michigan Archives, Record group 60-19, Box 1.

19. Charles W. Garfield to James B. Angell, December 14, 1908, State of Michigan Archives, Lansing.

CHAPTER 3. GETTING ORGANIZED, 1907–1909

1. *Report of the Commission of Inquiry, Tax Lands and Forestry, to the Governor and Legislature of the State* (Lansing, Mich.: Wynkoop, Hallenbeck, Crawford, 1908), 51–52.

2. Ibid., 108.

3. Ibid., 10.

4. Ibid., 102.

5. *Report of the Commission of Inquiry*, 104.

6. Ibid., 103.

7. Ibid., 101.

8. Ibid.

9. Ibid., 102.

10. Ibid., 117.

11. Ibid., 11.

12. Ibid., 108.

13. Ibid., 20.

14. Ibid., 22.

15. William B. Mershon to J. H. Bissell, December 21, 1908, Mershon Papers, Bentley Historical Library, University of Michigan, Ann Arbor.

16. *Report of the Commission of Inquiry*, 36–37.
17. *Report of the Commission of Inquiry*, 38.

CHAPTER 4. CUSTODIAL MANAGEMENT, 1909–1920

1. Michigan Public Domain Commission, *Proceedings*, 1909–10, 26, 80.
2. Ibid., 26, 85–87.
3. Ibid., 1910–11, 105.
4. Public Act 280, 1909.
5. Michigan Public Domain Commission, *Proceedings*, 1909–10, 27.
6. Ibid., 42.
7. Ibid., 68.
8. Ibid., 76.
9. Ibid., 77.
10. Ibid., 122–23.
11. Ibid., 130.
12. Ibid., 180.
13. Ibid., 1910–11, 98.
14. Ibid., 88.
15. Ibid., 82–95.
16. Ibid., 92–95, 112–13.
17. Michigan Public Domain Commission, *Proceedings*, 1912–13, 134.
18. Ibid., 1913–14, 16.
19. Ibid., 1915–16, 333–41, 525.
20. Ibid., 1916–17, 299–300.
21. Ibid., 86, 693.
22. Ibid., 1910–11, 75–76.
23. Ibid., 1914–15, 32, 48
24. Ibid., 1915–16, 81.
25. Ibid., 693.
26. Ibid., 1916–17, 234.
27. Ibid., 1918–19, 125, 63–64.
28. Ibid., 1917–18, 64, 135.
29. Ibid., 1917–18, 4.
30. Ibid., 55–56.
31. Ibid., 1918–19, 18.
32. Ibid., 1919–20, 488, 581.
33. Ibid., 639.
34. Ibid., 1917–18, 314.

Chapter 5. State Government Reorganization, 1921–1930

1. *Michigan Sportsman*, January, 1920, 7.
2. Ibid., 9.
3. Ibid., 12.
4. Ibid., 12.
5. Ibid., 13.
6. George Madsen, personal communication, 1968.
7. P. S. Lovejoy, "Plant Timber Crops, Expert's Suggestion," *Detroit News*, May 24, 1920, 1.
8. Fred Janette, "Would Avert Forest Fires," *Detroit News*, May 31, 1920, 8.
9. *American Forestry* 27, no. 333 (September 1921): 562.
10. Woodford, *Alex J. Groesbeck*, 127.
11. Michigan Department of Conservation *Proceedings*, 1921, 92.
12. *Michigan Forestry Association Newsletter*, March 1, 1925, 9.
13. Ibid., 10.
14. Michigan Department of Conservation, *Biennial Report*, 1923–24, 178.
15. David R. Jones, "Michigan's Reindeer Herd Transferred," *Michigan Sportsman*, February 15, 1923, 18.
16. Michigan Department of Conservation, *Proceedings*, 1924–25, 847.
17. Michigan Department of Conservation, *Biennial Report*, 1927–28, 333.
18. Michigan Department of Conservation, *Biennial Report*, 1921–22, 197, 203.
19. Michigan Department of Conservation, *Biennial Report*, 1925–26, 35.
20. Michigan Department of Conservation, *Biennial Report*, 1923–24, 178.
21. Michigan Department of Conservation, *Biennial Report*, 1925–26, 402.
22. Michigan Department of Conservation, *Biennial Report*, 1923–24, 178.
23. Michigan Department of Conservation, *Biennial Report*, 1929–30, 154.

Chapter 6. The Great Depression, 1931–1940

1. Michigan Forestry Association, *Newsletter,* September 6, 1930.
2. Michigan Department of Conservation, *Biennial Report*, 1931–32, 7.
3. Ibid., 7, 12.
4. Ibid., 13.
5. Ibid., 14.
6. Ibid., 175.
7. Ibid., 100.
8. Michigan Department of Conservation, *Biennial Report*, 1933–34, 213.
9. Ibid., 201.
10. Ibid., 213.
11. Ibid., 201.

12. Ibid., 213.
13. Ibid., 201.
14. Ibid., 213.
15. Michigan Department of Conservation, *Biennial Report*, 1935–36, 43.
16. Michigan Department of Conservation, internal memos, Archives, State of Michigan, Lansing.
17. Ibid.
18. Ibid.
19. Michigan Department of Conservation, *Biennial Report*, 1935–36, 6,7; Michigan Department of Conservation, *Biennial Report*, 1939–40, 206.
20. "Gov't to Buy Land in Allegan Co.," *Plainwell Enterprise*, April 4, 1935, 1.
21. "35,000 Acres to be Put in Forest Reserve in County," *Plainwell Enterprise*, October 31, 1935, 1.
22. Michigan Department of Conservation, *Biennial Report*, 1939–40, 286.
23. R. E. Trippensee, Wildlife Management: Upland Game and General Principles (New York: McGraw-Hill, 1948), 1:189.
24. Michigan Department of Conservation, *Biennial Report*, 1935–36, 178.
25. Michigan Department of Conservation, *Biennial Report*, 1937–38, 9, 201.
26. Michigan Department of Conservation, *Biennial Report*, 1935–36, 174.
27. Ibid., 206, 231
28. Michigan Department of Conservation, *Biennial Report*, 1939–40, 8.
29. Ibid., 282.

Chapter 7. The War Years, 1941–1946

1. Michigan Department of Conservation, *Biennial Report*, 1941–42, 7.
2. Michigan Department of Conservation, *Biennial Report*, 1941–42, 9.
3. Michigan Department of Conservation, *Proceedings*, 1942–43, 1.
4. Michigan Department of Conservation, *Biennial Report*, 1943–44, 100.
5. Ibid., 1941–42, 11.
6. Ibid., 295.
7. Ibid., 1943–44, 110–11.
8. Ibid., 111.
9. Ibid., 295.
10. Michigan Department of Conservation, *Biennial Report*, 1941–42, 8, 295.
11. Michigan Department of Conservation, *Proceedings*, 1942–43, 369.
12. Ibid., 40–43.
13. Norman F. Smith, "A Study of the Spread of Forest Cover into Wild Land Openings," *Papers of the Michigan Academy of Science, Arts and Letters* 28 (1942): 269–77.
14. Michigan Department of Conservation, *Biennial Report*, 1941–42, 314.
15. Ibid., 1943–44, 102.

16. Michigan Department of Conservation, *Proceedings*, 1941–42, 100–102.
17. Michigan Department of Conservation, *Biennial Report*, 1941–42, 315.
18. Ibid., 696–97, 237.
19. Michigan Department of Conservation, *Proceedings*, 1941–42, 370, 711.
20. Michigan Department of Conservation, *Biennial Report*, 1941–42, 243, 247.
21. Ibid., 249–52.
22. Ibid., 1943–44, 9–10.

CHAPTER 8. POSTWAR DEVELOPMENT, 1946–1958

1. Michigan Department of Conservation, *Biennial Report*, 1945–46, 11.
2. Michigan Department of Conservation, *Proceedings*, 1945–46, 500.
3. Ibid., 548.
4. Ibid., 548.
5. Ibid., 551.
6. Ibid., 552.
7. Michigan Department of Conservation, *Biennial Report*, 1945–46, 12.
8. Ibid., 14.
9. Ibid., 95.
10. Donald Zettle, conversation with author, Marquette, Mich., October 13, 2001.
11. Jack Van Coevering, "New Plan for Managing State's Game and Forest Lands," *Detroit Free Press*, April 7, 1946.
12. Michigan Department of Conservation, *Biennial Report*, 1945–46, 113.
13. Michigan Department of Conservation, *Proceedings*, 1948–49, 307–8.
14. Ibid., 1954–55, 116–17.
15. Michigan Department of Conservation, *Biennial Report*, 1959–60, 116.
16. Ibid., 117.
17. Michigan Department of Conservation, *Proceedings*, 1952–53, 1–2.
18. Ibid., 1954–55, 47–55.
19. Ibid.
20. Michigan Department of Conservation, *Biennial Report*, 1947–48, 126.
21. Ibid., 1949–50, 145.
22. Michigan Department of Conservation, *Proceedings*, 1953–54, 90.
23. Michigan Department of Conservation, *Biennial Report*, 1949–50, 146.
24. Ibid., 1951–52, 125.
25. Ibid., 1949–50, 138.
26. Michigan Department of Conservation, *Proceedings*, 1953–54, 88–92.
27. State of Michigan, Budget for the Fiscal Year ending June 30, 1954–55, vi; State of Michigan, Budget for the Fiscal Year ending June 30, 1955–56, vii; State of Michigan, Budget for the Fiscal Year ending June 30, 1956–57, vii.
28. Michigan Department of Conservation, *Biennial Report*, 1947–48, 121.

29. Ibid., 7.
30. Michigan Department of Conservation, *Proceedings*, 1953–54, 130.
31. Michigan Department of Conservation, *Proceedings*, 1954–55, 32.
32. Michigan Department of Conservation, *Biennial Report*, 1949–50, 133.
33. Ibid., 1957–58, 120.
34. Michigan Department of Conservation, *Proceedings*, 1956–57, 291.
35. Michigan Department of Conservation, *Biennial Report*, 1949–50, 158–59.
36. James L. Halbach, personal communication, 1966.
37. Michigan Department of Conservation, *Biennial Report*, 1949–50, 138.
38. Ibid., 1955–56, 118–19, 1957–58, 123–24, 1959–60.
39. Ibid., 1947–48, 146.
40. Ibid., 1955–56, 118.
41. Ibid., 1957–58, 123–24.
42. Ibid., 1951–52, 113.
43. Ibid., 1953–54, 143.
44. Ibid., 1949–50, 159.
45. Ibid., 1951–52, 135–37.
46. Ibid., 1953–54, 144–45.
47. Ibid., 146.
48. Ibid., 1959–60, 127.
49. Ibid., 1951–52, 133–35.
50. Michigan Department of Natural Resources files, Lansing.
51. Michigan Department of Conservation, *Biennial Report*, 1951–52, 127.
52. Ibid., 1953–54, 135.
53. Ibid., 1949–50, 180.
54. Ibid., 1952–53, 134–35.
55. Michigan Department of Conservation, *Proceedings*, 1947–48, 146–50.
56. Michigan Department of Conservation, *Biennial Report*, 1949–50, 177–78.
57. James C. Lamy to Ronald G. Auble, August 5, 1954, Department of Natural Resources files.
58. Ford Kellum to James C. Lamy, August 24, 1954, Department of Natural Resources files.
59. Fred H. Haskin to Ronald G. Auble, August 28, 1961, Department of Natural Resources files.
60. Michigan Department of Conservation, *Biennial Report*, 1949–50, 159, 175.
61. Ibid., 1953–54, 137.
62. Kenneth McCormick, "State Hearing to Air Charge of Irregularity in Conservation Department," *Detroit Free Press*, December 13, 1952, 1.
63. Ibid.
64. Ibid.
65. Kenneth McCormick, "Lumber Concerns Assail Wardens," *Detroit Free Press*, December 15, 1952.

66. "Free Press Expose Applauded," *Detroit Free Press*, December 15, 1952.

67. Kenneth McCormick, "2 Named in Timber Raids," *Detroit Free Press*, December 20, 1952, 1.

68. Michigan Department of Conservation, *Proceedings*, 1952–53, 231–32.

69. Ibid., 268–69; Michigan Department of Conservation, *Biennial Report*, 1951–52, 127–28.

70. Michigan Department of Conservation, *Proceedings*, 1952–53, 268–69.

71. Ibid., 1959–60, 117.

72. Ibid., 97.

73. Ibid., 115.

74. Michigan Department of Conservation, *Proceedings*, 1953–54, 92.

75. Michigan Department of Conservation, *Biennial Report*, 1951–52, 113.

76. Ibid., 1955–56, 98; Michigan Department of Conservation, *Proceedings*, 1956–57, 112, 254.

77. Ibid., 192.

78. Michigan Department of Conservation, *Biennial Report*, 1959–60, 101.

79. Ibid., 1957–58, 104.

80. Ibid., 1955–56, 110.

81. Ibid., 1959–60, 128.

82. Ibid.

83. Michigan Department of Conservation, *Proceedings*, 1949–50, 349–50.

84. Ibid., 1954–55, 226.

85. Ibid., 1954–55, 226.

86. Michigan Department of Conservation, *Biennial Report*, 1957–58, 99.

CHAPTER 9. THE FULLY MANAGED, MULTIPLE-USE FOREST ERA, 1959–1975

1. Michigan Department of Conservation, *Proceedings*, 1960–61, 286–87.

2. Ibid.

3. Michigan Department of Conservation, *Biennial Report*, 1961–62, finance-l, forestry-l.

4. Michigan Department of Conservation, *Proceedings*, 1961–62, 53, 77.

5. Ibid., 112–13.

6. Michigan Department of Conservation, *Biennial Report*, 1961–62, forestry-l.

7. Ibid.

8. Ibid., 19–20.

9. Michigan Department of Conservation, *Biennial Report*, 1961–62, 29; Frank W. Kearns, Lee M. James, Norman F. Smith, and Ray E. Pfeifer, *An Economic Appraisal of Michigan's State Forests* (Lansing: Forestry Division, Michigan Department of Conservation, 1962).

10. Michigan Department of Conservation, *Proceedings*, 1961–62, 384.

11. Michigan Department of Conservation, *Biennial Report*, 1961–62, forestry-2.
12. Ibid., 30.
13. Michigan Department of Conservation, *Proceedings*, 1962–63, 135–36.
14. Michigan Department of Conservation, *Biennial Report*, 1961–62, 18.
15. Ibid., 18.
16. Ibid., 263.
17. Ibid., 30.
18. Michigan Department of Conservation, *Proceedings*, 1962–63, 198–99.
19. Michigan Department of Conservation, *Biennial Report*, 1963–64, 10.
20. Ibid.
21. Ibid., 1965–66, 11.
22. Ibid.
23. Michigan Department of Conservation, *Proceedings*, 1964–65, 2.
24. Paul R. Flink, personal communication, ca. 1980.
25. Michigan Department of Conservation, *Proceedings*, 1963–64, 309.
26. Michigan Department of Conservation, *Biennial Report*, 1965–66, 55.
27. Michigan Department of Conservation, *Biennial Report*, 1965–66, 65.
28. Ibid., 1967–68, 24.
29. Michigan Department of Conservation, *Biennial Report*, 1965–66, 66.
30. Ibid., 58.
31. Michigan Department of Natural Resources, *Biennial Report*, 1969–70, 62.
32. Michigan Department of Conservation, *Biennial Report*, 1967–68, 58.
33. Ibid., 1965–66, 69.
34. Michigan Department of Natural Resources, *Biennial Report*, 1969–70, 65.
35. Michigan Department of Natural Resources, *Biennial Report*, 1969–70, 54.
36. Ibid., 1971–72, 9.
37. Ibid., 1971–72, 67, 78.
38. Michigan Department of Natural Resources, *Proceedings*, 1971–72, 528–29.
39. Michigan Department of Natural Resources, *Biennial Report*, 1971–72, 528–29.
40. Ibid., 1971–72, 67.
41. Ibid., 1979–80, 45.
42. Michigan Department of Natural Resources, *Proceedings*, 1972–73, 263.
43. Ibid., 1972–73, 403–4.
44. Ibid., 1973–74, 7.
45. Ibid., 1972–73, 319.
46. Ibid., 1974–75, 113.
47. Ibid., 1969–70, 483.
48. Ibid., 1970–71, 97–98.
49. Ibid., 1972–73, 261–62.
50. Ibid., 1972–73, 205, 545.
51. Ibid., 1973–74, 216–17; ibid., 1975–76, 119–20.
52. Ibid., 1974–75, 57.

53. Ibid., 1973–74, 9–13.
54. Ibid., 1970–71, 98–99.
55. Ibid., 1970–71, 125.
56. Ibid., 1970–71, 503.
57. Ibid., 1972–73, 3.
58. Ibid., 1972–73, 462–63.
59. Michigan Department of Natural Resources, *Biennial Report*, 1973–74, 72.
60. Michigan Department of Natural Resources, *Proceedings*, 1970–71, 281-82.
61. Michigan Department of Natural Resources, *Biennial Report*, 1973–74, 279.
62. Ibid., 1971–72, 78.
63. Personal communications with the author, October 31, 2002.
64. Michigan Department of Natural Resources, *Biennial Report*, 1973–74, 71.
65. Ibid., 1975–76, 188 .
66. Ibid., 1969–70, 89.
67. Michigan Department of Natural Resources, Commission minutes of December 9–10, 1976, 57–58.
68. Michigan Department of Natural Resources, *Biennial Report*, 1979–80, 136.
69. Ibid., 1979–80, 136.
70. Michigan Department of Natural Resources, *Proceedings*, 1973–74, 357–58.

CHAPTER 10. FOREST RESOURCE PLANNING, 1975–1990

1. Michigan Department of Natural Resources, minutes, October 1975, 63.
2. Ibid., January 1976, 116.
3. Ibid., February 12–13, 1976, 5.
4. Michigan Department of Natural Resources, *Biennial Report*, 1973–74, 74–75.
5. Ibid.
6. Russell Hellman, personal communication, February 8, 1977.
7. James Bielecki, telephone conversation, October 17, 2002.
8. Michigan Department of Natural Resources, minutes, June 9–10, 1977, 2; *Michigan Timber Resource Development Project*.
9. *Michigan Timber Resource Development Project*.
10. Ibid., 9.
11. Ibid., 21–22.
12. Michigan Department of Natural Resources, minutes, July 14–15, 1977, 2.
13. Ibid., 4.
14. Ibid., 16.
15. Ibid., March 9–10, 1978, 2–3.
16. Ibid., April 13–14, 1978, 4.
17. Marion Clawson, *Forests for Whom and for What?* (Baltimore: Johns Hopkins University Press for Resources for the Future, 1975).

18. Michigan Department of Natural Resources, *Biennial Report*, 1979–80, 38.
19. Michigan Department of Natural Resources, minutes, January 1984, 4–9.
20. Ibid., September 12–13, 1984, 6.
21. Ibid., July 6–7, 1988, 2–3.
22. Ibid., September 7–8, 1978, 12.
23. Ibid., February 9–10, 1984, 13.
24. Ibid., October 10–11, 1984, 2.
25. Michigan Department of Natural Resources, minutes, July, 1983, 5–7.

CHAPTER 11. ECOSYSTEM MANAGEMENT AND BIODIVERSITY, 1991–2005

1. Gerald Thiede, conversation with authors, December 5, 2002.
2. John Engler, news release, November 8, 1991.
3. Michigan Department of Natural Resources, minutes, October 9–10, 1991, 6.
4. Ibid., April 10–11, 1991, 7.
5. Michigan Department of Natural Resources, minutes, August 12–13, 1992, 10.
6. Ibid., July 10–11, 1991, 4.
7. Ibid., October 7–8, 1992, 11.
8. Ibid., May 12–13, 1993, 13–15.
9. Michael Paluda, personal communication, January 29, 2003.
10. Bill Botti, "State of the State Forests," *Michigan Forests* 10, no. 1 (1989): 6.
11. Michigan Department of Natural Resources, minutes, July 25, 1991, 2–3; August 14, 1991, 3.
12. Michigan Department of Natural Resources, minutes, September 9–10, 1992, 5, 7, September 7–8, 1994, 8.
13. Michael Paluda, personal communication, January 29, 2003.
14. Michigan Department of Natural Resources, minutes, August 12–13, 1992, 8.
15. Ibid., February 10–11, 1993, 2–6.
16. Ibid., March 4, 1993, 3–5.
17. Ibid., March 10–11, 1993, 3–4.
18. Ibid., 11.
19. Thiede, conversation with authors; Michigan Department of Natural Resources, minutes, April 14–15, 1993, 19.
20. Ada Takacs, telephone conversation with author, December 20, 2002.
21. Michigan Department of Natural Resources, minutes, May 12–13, 1993, 15.
22. Takacs, telephone conversation with author.
23. Thiede, conversation with authors.
24. Michigan Department of Natural Resources, minutes, April 13–14, 1994, 3.
25. Ibid., June 8–9, 1994, 5, 15–16.
26. File 94-77725-AA, February 8, 1994, Judge William Collette, Michigan Department of Attorney General.

27. Michigan Department of Natural Resources, minutes, September 6–7, 1995, 34–52.
28. Department of Natural Resources files, Lansing.
29. Thiede, conversation with authors.
30. Michigan Department of Natural Resources, minutes, June 4–5, 1997, 5.
31. Michigan Department of Natural Resources, minutes, April 8–9, 1998, 6–7.
32. Ibid., May 13–14, 1998, 1–2, 4.
33. Ibid., June 10–11, 1998, 7–8.
34. Michigan Department of Natural Resources, minutes, April 12, 1995, 4–5.
35. Ibid., December 1996, 3–5.
36. Ibid., December 6–7, 2000, 8.
37. Ibid., November 3–4, 1999, 3–4.
38. Ibid., February 8–9, 2001, 11.
39. Ibid., December 6–7, 2000, 5–6.
40. Mindy Koch, interview with author, September 10, 2001.
41. Department of Natural Resources News Release, "State of Michigan Earns Dual Forest Certification," January 12, 2006.
42. Michigan Department of Natural Resources, minutes, April 11–12, 2002, 2–3.

Epilogue

1. Neil deGrasse Tyson, "Naming Rights: How to Stake a Claim in the Dictionary of Science," *Natural History* 112 (February, 2003): 24–46.

Appendix. What's in a Name?

1. Michigan Department of Conservation, *Biennial Report*, 1963–64, 10.

Bibliography

MANUSCRIPT COLLECTIONS

Michigan Historical Collections, Bentley Historical Library, University of Michigan, Ann Arbor
Curwood, James Oliver. Papers
Garfield, Charles W. Papers
Lovejoy, Parish Storrs. Papers
Roth, Filibert. Papers

NEWSPAPERS, PERIODICALS, AND JOURNALS

Allegan News
American Forestry (later *American Forests and Forest Life* and *American Forests*)
Country Gentleman
Crawford County Avalanche
Detroit Free Press
Detroit News
Journal of Forestry
Michigan Conservation
Michigan Forestry Association Newsletter
Michigan History
Michigan Natural Resources Magazine
Michigan Out-of-Doors Magazine
Michigan Sportsman
Natural History

Natural Science
Northwoods Call
Plainwell Enterprise
Roscommon Herald-News
Roscommon News

GOVERNMENT DOCUMENTS

Allen, Clifford, ed. *Michigan Log Marks, Their Function and Use during the Great Michigan Pine Harvest.* East Lansing: Michigan State College Agricultural Experiment Station, 1941.

Daw, T. E. *Michigan State Forests: For Wildlife, Commerce, Recreation.* Lansing: Michigan Department of Conservation, 1961.

Foster, Helen, comp. and ed. *1921–1946: Twenty-five Years of Conservation in Michigan.* Lansing: Michigan Department of Conservation, Office of Information and Education, 1960.

Michigan Board of Agriculture. *Annual Reports.* various dates, 1888.

Michigan Forestry Commission. *Annual Reports* and minutes. 1889–91, 1899–1908.

Michigan Department of Conservation. *Proceedings of Conservation Commission.* 1921–63.

Michigan Department of Natural Resources. *Proceedings* and minutes. 1964–2005.

Michigan Public Domain Commission. *Proceedings.* 1909–20.

Michigan Timber Resource Development Project: Pre-Feasibility Report, Vol. 1, *Forestry.* Lansing: Forestry Division, Michigan Department of Natural Resources, 1977.

Michigan's Forest Resources: Direction for the Future: A Statewide Forest Resources Plan. Lansing: Michigan Department of Natural Resources, 1983.

Mitchell, J. A., and D. Robson. *Forest Fires and Forest Fire Control in Michigan.* Lansing: Michigan Department of Conservation in cooperation with United States Department of Agriculture, Forest Service, 1950.

Mitchell, J. A., and H. R. Sayre. *Forest Fires in Michigan.* Lansing: Michigan Department of Conservation, 1931.

Moore, Michael D., ed. *Proceedings of Governor James J. Blanchard's Conference on Forest Resources: Creating 50,000 New Jobs in Michigan Forest Products Industries, Including Recommendations and Responses.* East Lansing: Michigan State University, 1983.

Proceedings of Governor William G. Milliken's Forestry Conference: Including Recommendations and Responses. Houghton: Michigan Technological University, 1980.

Proposed Old Growth and Biodiversity Stewardship Planning Process and Draft Criteria for Michigan's State Forests and Other State Owned Lands: A Report from the Michigan Department of Natural Resources. Lansing: Michigan Department of Natural Resources, 2001.

Rosentreter, Roger L. *Roosevelt's Tree Army: Michigan's Civilian Conservation Corps.* Lansing: Michigan Department of State, 1986.

Smith, Norman F. *Michigan Forests and Forestry.* Lansing: Michigan Department of Conservation, 1947.

Titus, Harold. *The Land Nobody Wanted: The Story of Michigan's Public Domain.* East Lansing: Michigan State College, Agricultural Experiment Station, Section of Conservation, 1945.

PUBLISHED SOURCES

Dempsey, David. *Ruin and Recovery: Michigan's Rise as a Conservation Leader.* Ann Arbor: University of Michigan Press, 2001.

Dickmann, Donald I., and Larry A. Leefers. *The Forests of Michigan.* Ann Arbor: University of Michigan Press, 2003.

Floyd, Donald W. *Forest Sustainability: The History, the Challenge, the Promise.* Durham, N.C.: Forest History Society, 2002.

Gough, Robert. *Farming the Cutover: A Social History of Northern Wisconsin, 1900–1940.* Lawrence: University Press of Kansas, 1997.

Kates, James. *Planning a Wilderness: Regenerating the Great Lakes Cutover Region.* Minneapolis: University of Minnesota Press, 2001.

MacCleery, Douglas W. *American Forests: A History of Resiliency and Recovery.* Durham, N.C.: U.S. Department of Agriculture, in cooperation with Forest History Society, 1993.

Mershon, William B. *Recollections of My Fifty Years Hunting and Fishing.* Boston: Stratford, 1923.

Pinchot, Gifford. *Breaking New Ground.* New York: Harcourt, Brace, 1947.

———. *The Conservation Diaries of Gifford Pinchot.* Ed. Harold K. Steen. Durham, N.C.: Forest History Society, 2001.

Robbins, William G. *American Forestry: A History of National, State, and Private Cooperation.* Lincoln: University of Nebraska Press, 1985.

Shands, William E., ed. *The Lake States Forests: A Resources Renaissance.* St. Paul, Minn.: Lake States Forestry Alliance, 1988.

Symon, Charles A. *We Can Do It!: A History of the Civilian Conservation Corps in Michigan, 1933–1942.* Gladstone, Mich.: Symon, 1983.

Titus, Harold. *"Timber."* Boston: Small, Maynard, 1922.

Verme, Louis J. *Forestry Schools in Upper Michigan: Then and Now.* Munising, Mich.: Avanti, 1999.

Widner, Ralph, ed. *Forests and Forestry in the American States: A Reference Anthology.* Missoula, Mont.: National Association of State Foresters, 1968.

Woodford, Frank B. *Alex J. Groesbeck: Portrait of a Public Man.* Detroit: Wayne State University Press, 1962.